PRAISE FOR AUTHOR KEN LAVIGNE AND HIS BOOK *COACH THE SOUL*

"I've had the opportunity to travel the world, asking young folks and old, the wealthy and the poor, the famous and the infamous, to tell me about their favorite teacher. I never hear stories about teachers that have to do with curriculum or content standards. I never hear about pretty classrooms or PowerPoint presentations. I never hear about grades or report cards, back-to-school nights or special field trips. What do I hear about? I hear about soul.

"Coach Ken LaVigne is a teacher with soul. He is one of the best educators you'll ever meet. He looks deep inside his students to search for their unique and beautiful potential. Pushing past tragedy and the terrible choices young people can make: violence, drug use, family chaos, poverty, and despair, he goes to work gently, persistently, passionately pulling the best out of the young men and women he teaches. This book, crafted from the gritty stories of the real kids he teaches and the formative experiences from his own life, tells you everything you need to know about how to become that one person who makes a difference in the lives of others. It will also show you how important it is to know and nurture the souls of the children we are entrusted with teaching, for that has the power to change everything.

"They say that for children to make it, they just need one person, one person in their lives who believes in them, who won't ever give up, and who makes the journey with them to ensure they make it. For hundreds, if not thousands of kids, Coach LaVigne is that person. This book will show you why."

~ **Rebecca Mieliwocki**
2012 National Teacher of the Year

"Ken LaVigne is a truly remarkable educator, and his passion and expertise shines brightly in **Coach the Soul**. His stories, reflections, and advice will make you a better teacher and a more complete human being. There is wisdom on every page."

~ **Alex Kajitani**
Speaker, Author & 2009 California State Teacher of the Year

"Ken LaVigne is a gifted and talented writer. His stories should be shared with new educators as they enter our profession. These new teachers really need to understand the power of relationships, learning about their kids, and the power they have to change lives. They need to understand what an important force they are in the lives of the students they see every day.

"This is one of the most heart-wrenching and uplifting books I have ever read. I cried, my heart swelled with pride, and this book left me inspired. Not only can I see the quilt that his grandmother made in my mind's eye, but also the quilt that he has created with the stories of his students and the many lives he has touched. It is so important for us as educators to remember that we teach CHILDREN, children who have a story, a story that they are sometimes afraid to share. Once they feel our hearts, they will share theirs with us."

~ **Helen Papadopoulos**
2007 California State Teacher of the Year

"Ken's heroic tales of the many vulnerable and at-risk students, whose lives have been deeply touched by him through his unique educational program, present just one piece of the scope of his program's influence.

"As an Advanced Placement English teacher and College Counselor at La Serna High School, I worked with a number of the students who served as mentors for Ken's OASIS students. They labored in his classroom daily to provide motivation, emotional and academic support, and importantly, to serve as role models. Many mentors shared their personal experiences in the OASIS program in their college application essays. They wrote of the humility and respect that came from working with students, many of whom had desperately challenging life circumstances to endure. They wrote of an awakened appreciation for their own teachers, gained from experiencing first-hand the difficulty of motivating and inspiring students who are reluctant to learn. They wrote of the satisfaction and reward that came from forging a personal and meaningful relationship with a peer they would probably not, otherwise, have gotten to know. They wrote of the deep and abiding love and respect they had for "Coach" LaVigne as they watched him coax, cajole, encourage, demand, support, and love the students he was often pulling or pushing toward a successful academic finish line. The life lessons they shared in their college applications were often as deep and as powerful as those of the students they helped to coach.

"Shortly after Ken was hired to teach and coach football at La Serna, our principal, Leo Camalich, asked me if I had met Ken yet. When I answered that I hadn't, he said, reflectively, "You'll like him. He is the kind of person people just like to be around." Ken's innate humility causes him to deflect any personal accolades. He is always quick to point to the efforts of others who work with and around him. *Coach the Soul* demonstrates how one man's—one educator's—personal commitment to the success of every single student to both endure and prevail can happen through embracing the core values of the human soul."

~ **Karen Lantz**
Advanced Placement English Teacher,
College and Career Advisor, La Serna High School

"The tapestry of stories in *Coach the Soul* positively influences the reader as teachers and mentors make the difference in the lives of so many. The heartfelt honesty and life stories are candid and express the wonderful spirit of humankind. I have worked with author Ken LaVigne for over twenty-five years, and his gift of storytelling is an absolute treasure."

~ **Dina Tsuyuki**
English Teacher and Department Chair, La Serna High School

"Before meeting Ken LaVigne and being a mentor in the OASIS program, I was set on my career choice to be a neuroscientist. After my two years as an OASIS mentor and getting to work with Mr. LaVigne, I am currently pursuing my teaching credential. *Coach the Soul* is a privilege and an honor to read. Knowing what it is like in that classroom with Mr. LaVigne, I understand how true these stories are. I am so grateful to know Ken LaVigne, to have learned from him, and to have been inspired by him. While reading this book, I don't think my eyes stopped watering for even a second. It is a gift to educators everywhere; truly it is! It fills your heart to the brim. Teaching is less about history and math, and much more about coaching the soul."

~ **Emily Brock**
Two-Year OASIS Academic Mentor, La Serna High School

"Coach Ken LaVigne is one of the individuals I admire most in this world. I am truly thankful to have him in my life and am honored to call him my friend. Over the years, he has inspired me to be a better man and coach. He continues to be my role model to this day. For me, it feels like all is well with the world each time I have the opportunity to enjoy his company. He has a special gift of making people feel good about themselves. *Coach the Soul* paints an incredible picture of the life of a great man who has inspired so many. What an awesome journey it has been! Thank you, Coach. I hope you know how much you mean to me and my family"

~ **Andy George**
Head Varsity Football Coach, Teacher, La Serna High School

"Ken LaVigne is as rare of a person that you will ever meet. His authentic and personal touch to *Coach the Soul* is his lifelong journey as a professional educator. This book is a must-read for anyone and will inspire those looking to make a difference in the lives of America's youth. Mentoring not only the youth, he touched my own life and helped shape the person and coach I am today."

~ **Dave Pierson**
Head Varsity Football Coach, Teacher, Santa Fe High School

"*Coach the Soul* takes you on a journey inside the heart of what it is to be a great teacher. Ken LaVigne's passion and commitment to students who have given up on themselves is a testament to the power of unconditional love. It also demonstrates that the more you give, the more you receive; for as much as Ken has changed the lives of these students, his soul has been indelibly inked by their kindness and gratitude. It is a powerful story of what is possible when you 'teach their minds but most importantly, coach their souls.'"

~ **Martin Plourde**
Superintendent, Whittier Union High School District

"Ken LaVigne's *Coach the Soul* shares the experiences of resilient high school at-risk students to life in this collection of inspirational stories. Ken and the student mentors that he trains are bridge builders who repair human souls. This book will open eyes and hearts alike to the journey that so many of our young people today are forced to make."

~ **Lisa Barnes**
Intervention Specialist, La Serna High School

"Ken,
It is 12:30 am and I just finished reading your manuscript. I started it this morning when I had a few minutes before my day got started and I couldn't wait to get back to it this evening! My eyes are blurry from reading on my iPad in the dark but they are also moist with the tears I shed while reading this beautiful patchwork quilt you have created! Thank you from the bottom of my heart for sharing this book with me. Thank you for the important role you played in the life of my boys! I cannot wait until it is available in print as I have already started my list of people that I plan to buy it for! Thanks so much!"

~ **Tracy Fish**

"I have known Coach LaVigne since 1997 when he arrived at La Serna. He was my son Stephen's head coach and line coach for the varsity football team. At the beginning of the season, Stephen came home from practice with his game jersey. It was number 55. Stephen had played football for the past three years, two years with La Serna and a year in Pop Warner. His number was always 50, so I was upset Stephen was not given the number 50 now that he was starting on the varsity football team. I told Stephen I was going to go to the coach and get his number changed. Stephen told me to calm down and said that each year, Coach LaVigne secretly gives a lineman who he truly respects the number 55 because that was Coach's number. That player would be an extension of Coach LaVigne on the field. It is a sign of deep respect and trust. I spoke to Coach about this and he asked me if I would like to change Stephen's number. He said that it was my decision. That demonstrated to me the character of the man Coach Ken LaVigne. He is my brother from another mother. I love him."

~ **Claudine Sanchez-Parrott**

"I have had the personal and professional privilege of working with Ken LaVigne for more than twenty years. I consider him one of my heroes. In *Coach the Soul*, Ken very poignantly demonstrates that when you lead with the heart, then and only then do people feel valued, and that's when the learning begins. Ken or "Coach" as we loving call him, reminds us that we are all complicated human beings and it is through our real connections to one another that we all become better people. *Coach the Soul* is sure to inspire and quite possibly move you to impact the life of another."

~ **Ann Fitzgerald**
Principal, La Serna High School

"Over the past 26 years, I have had the privilege of getting to know Ken LaVigne on many levels. First, as his student at Santa Fe High School, later teaching alongside him in our Intervention program at La Serna, and currently as an administrator continuing to work closely with our OASIS program. *Coach the Soul* compiles genuine stories of challenges and triumphs that Ken and his students have experienced over the years within and outside of the classroom. These stories are told by a man who wears his huge heart on his sleeve, and teaches even the most at-risk students that it's okay to do so as well. This book reveals inspiring scenarios that demonstrate the hope and grit that Ken expends on a daily basis to make huge differences in the lives of his students and all who cross his path, including myself."

~ **Kristin Kooiman**
Former Student of Ken LaVigne,
Assistant Principal, Curriculum, La Serna High School

"*Coach the Soul,* depicting the journey that Ken LaVigne has taken from childhood, touches our hearts with every story that he shares. His own reflections on how he became the man he is today are heightened by his commitment to his students and his willingness to bring love and order to their lives. Their stories and the impact of Ken's embrace will inspire you. As hope resonates throughout this book, you will sing Ken's praises and feel determined that you, too, can make a difference in the lives of our most vulnerable youth."

~ **Rita Stevens**
Assistant Principal, Guidance,
La Serna High School

"*Coach the Soul* is a book that anyone can relate to and, without a doubt, is a must read for any educator, whether a seasoned veteran, first-year teacher, or anybody interested in learning to unconditionally love and show true compassion for their fellow man. Within the bindings, one not only gets a glimpse into being an educator but an understanding that being "Coach" is something far greater than only being in the classroom and applying theory and sticking to curriculum. It's about love, empathy, and compassion; and Ken LaVigne delivers his stories and teachings without constraints. I can do nothing but sing praise after praise not only for this book, but for the man, my coach and mentor, Ken LaVigne. Bravo, bravo!"

~ **Jimmy Hope**
Former Football Player and Student of Ken LaVigne,
English Teacher, Whittier High School

COACH
THE SOUL

Ken LaVigne

Robert D. Reed Publishers . Bandon, OR

Robert D. Reed Publishers
P.O. Box 1992
Bandon, OR 97411
Phone: 541-347-9882; Fax: -9883
E-mail: 4bobreed@msn.com
Website: www.rdrpublishers.com

Editor: Cleone Reed
Book Designer: Amy Cole
Cover Designer: Ron Imada

13 Digit ISBN 978-944297-36-7
eBook: ISBN 978-944297-37-4

Library of Congress Number: 2018954169

Designed and Formatted in the United States of America

DEDICATION

To my mother and father, the best coaches I ever had. Your unselfish dedication to our family is the standard for my life as a husband and a father. I love you and miss you every single day. Rest well in Heaven.

To Dick Torres, Jack Mahlstede, and Clint South, the heroes of my life, whose influence saved me and countless others.

To Clint, my first-born son, whose birth grounded me and whose life has inspired me. You are a source of incredible joy and pride for which I am eternally grateful. You will always be at the center of my heart.

To Mark, my younger son, personal protector, and guardian angel. You amaze me every day with your unselfish dedication and compassion for others. I am so proud to be the father of such a special young man.

And finally, To Gisele, my wife, best friend, and most trusted advisor. Your selfless loyalty through all these years is what kept me fighting and believing. Coming home to you is the best part of my day…every day.

NOTE:

I changed the names of almost all the students in this book so that I would not embarrass them or their families with private, sensitive details. Their names and faces are deeply etched in my mind and heart. They know who they are and so do I.

We are not saints, we are not heroes. Our lives are lived in the quiet corners of the ordinary. We build tiny hearth fires, sometimes barely strong enough to give off warmth. But to the person lost in the darkness, our tiny flame may be the road to safety, the path to salvation. It is not given us to know who is lost in the darkness that surrounds us or even if our light is seen. We can only know that against even the smallest of lights, darkness cannot stand. A sailor lost at sea can be guided home by a single candle. A person lost in a wood can be led to safety by a flickering flame. It is not an issue of quality or intensity or purity. It is simply an issue of the presence of light."

~ Kent Nerburn
Make Me an Instrument of Your Peace

CONTENTS

ACKNOWLEDGMENTS

Writing this book has been a journey that would never have been possible without some amazing people who led, supported, and inspired me along the way. Simply knowing them is a gift. Having them accompany me on this journey makes their gift priceless.

Raymond and Florida LaVigne, my beloved parents, are the most important influences in my life. I think about their unselfish love and constant encouragement every day. They always placed my needs ahead of their own, sacrificing so much to give me every opportunity possible.

Gisele, my beautiful wife and best friend, has always believed in me and supported me in everything I have ever done in our 35-year marriage. She is absolutely the best thing that ever happened to me.

This book would have never been written without the encouragement, persuasion, and persistence of my son Mark. He is an incredibly caring, giving, and talented human being. I am so proud to be his father!

Clint, my older son, sacrificed many hours and worked so hard to become an outstanding football player and an even better son for his proud father. He gave me precious memories of our time together, and I love him so very much.

Jack Mahlstede, Clint South, and Dick Torres were my coaches but so much more! They literally saved my life and made it richer by coaching my soul and making the life I enjoy possible.

Ron Imada, my friend of fifty years, is more like a brother than a friend. His skills and heart in creating my book cover is beyond special because he, too, is such a big part of my life.

Dick Cheung is a dear friend who volunteered his abilities as a photographer and made me look a lot better than what I really am. For that and his friendship, I am truly grateful.

Tim Traeger is a dedicated community leader and volunteer in our OASIS program who contributed photos for the book's cover. I am grateful and lucky to know him.

Karen Lantz, lovingly referred to as St. Karen in the LaVigne home because of her kind and nurturing spirit, was absolutely crucial in the completion of this book. For years, she was my primary editor, motivator, and the voice I listened to the most.

Dina Tsuyuki and Susan Verstegen, two of my most trusted friends, helped me greatly with their reading and honest reactions to the book as it evolved through the years.

Sandy Thorstenson is, quite simply, the finest leader and human being I have ever known. Her example of what it takes to be a good educator has always been the template I try to emulate as a teacher and coach. I am so proud and grateful to have her write the Foreword for my book!

Rebecca Mieliwocki, Alex Kajitani, Helen Papadopoulos, Martin Plourde, Lisa Barnes, Claudine Sanchez-Parrott, Tracy Fish, Emily Brock, Dave Pierson, Andy George, Ann Fitzgerald, Rita Stevens, Kristin Kooiman, and Jimmy Hope are extraordinary people for whom I have immense respect. Their endorsements of my book are treasures for which I will always be grateful.

Amy Cole used her tremendous skills in formatting this book. I am very grateful for her time, talent, and expertise.

Lisa Ceja, an extraordinary educator and outstanding leader in our school district, gave her technological brilliance as well as her supportive patience in designing the **Coach the Soul** website.

All my students, academic mentors, football players, fellow coaches, teachers, colleagues, and friends have had a profound influence on my life. I am blessed to know them and to have worked alongside them through the years. I don't think they realize what a powerful impact that they made on my life. Memories of them and what they have done along the way fill my heart and inspire me every single day.

Finally, Bob and Cleone Reed took a chance on me by publishing this book. They are uniquely genuine as well as skilled at their craft. Bob's wise and reassuring words have given me confidence in myself and what I have written. Cleone's dedicated and encouraging support as both an editor and advisor are more important and valuable than she will ever know. I am so lucky to know them!

FOREWORD

"**C**oach the Soul** has a message that should be absorbed by anyone who intends to enter the profession of education. Teachers are leaders. Anyone who is in any position to lead, whether in business, industry, community, or faith organizations, can benefit by Ken LaVigne's extraordinary model of effective leadership. By sharing the stories of some of the students whose lives he has touched in the classroom, Ken defines and demonstrates what a true, motivational leader looks like. He understands that success comes from the depth of an interpersonal approach rather than simple technical expertise. This is a book about the experiences of a successful teacher, but there is a lesson to be learned for anyone who is called to lead—that people of all ages flourish in an environment of compassion, respect, and support.

"When Ken agreed to spearhead the program for underachieving students at La Serna High School, he brought his football coaching skills, teaching expertise, and personal values into a challenging classroom environment. His students—many of whom face harrowing life circumstances and are also reluctant students—grow to respect the accountability he requires while enjoying and valuing the new sense of belonging. They learn that Ken's commitment to their success cannot be his alone, and he works hard to instill a sense of community, caring, and personal responsibility as well as to provide a safe haven in which to thrive.

"Ken recognizes that academic knowledge is only one piece of being a successful, productive person. **Coach the Soul** identifies, chapter by chapter, the qualities, characteristics, and values that are intrinsic to being a responsible, whole, valuable member of society. His illustrative stories and anecdotes demonstrate how to effectively recognize and to help instill those characteristics no matter the student's background. Ken has consistently proven that demographics do not determine destiny. It is the passionate teacher who has the greatest impact on a student's future.

"Serving in secondary education for 39 years, I have always been perplexed by those who cringe at the idea of actually choosing to work with high school students. Teenagers are astutely intuitive. They can sense authenticity and in the hands of a true educator and mentor and they can be motivated, inspired, and prepared to be caring, productive, informed citizens of the world. Ever the teacher and coach, Ken reinforces what matters most in effective teaching, coaching, and leading—treating students who are entrusted to us with respect, listening, caring, and demonstrating genuine compassion. And, importantly, he identifies the critical human and societal values, which are the necessary building blocks to becoming productive, responsible human beings.

"In *Coach the Soul*, Ken has shared his experience, his expertise, and the soul of what effective leadership—and good, solid teaching—should be."

~ **Sandy Thorstenson**
2012 California State Superintendent of the Year,
Superintendent Representative and Chair of the Board
of the California Collaborative for Educational Excellence

INTRODUCTION

DRAWING FROM
MY PERSONAL WELL

When I was a young boy and winter approached, my mother would get a wooden chair from the kitchen table and take it to the big closet in the middle of our small home. She set it carefully inside the closet, stood on it, and reached high for a quilt on the top shelf. She took the quilt down and laid it on my bed to keep me warm at night.

My grandmother made the quilt many years earlier when my mother was a young girl. It was beautiful! Small pieces of material that were all different were carefully sewn together to create a blanket that was both warm and comforting. Every year, my mother would tell me the same story about how her family was poor, had to struggle, and persevered through love and devotion to each other. Some of the pieces of fabric used on the quilt were ornate and of fine quality, material my grandmother had collected over time from others and saved to create her masterpiece. Other patches of fabric were scraps left over from homemade clothing sewn to save money. They were simple and not as fancy as others but they were also beautiful in their simplicity. Together, they made something magical that made me stare and wonder as I rubbed my hands across it as I waited for sleep to visit me at night.

My mother told me that the quilt was sewn together as much with love as it was with thread. It was an important part of who our family was and I should never forget that I was connected to something bigger than myself. That awareness sustained me as I grew up in a home filled with love but also filled with difficult times and turmoil.

This book is my quilt. It is a tapestry of lives that I have been lucky enough to know. I am not a young boy anymore, but an old man. The patches of material I use were given to me by young lives that blessed me with their own exquisite beauty. My quilt is sewn with memories of teenagers who made me stare and marvel at their strength, courage, and resilience to overcome adversity that I had never known existed before I met them. It is created with tears of sadness that were shed, as they told me stories of neglect, abuse, fear, and self-doubt. My pieces of fabric also include their tears of joy and accomplishment sprinkled with faces punctuated with hope. This is their masterpiece consecrated by their truly exceptional souls.

After almost thirty years of coaching football, I decided to retire as a coach but remain at my school as a teacher. Clint, my older son, had played football for me and his love of the sport fueled his willingness to make great sacrifices as the son of the head football coach. I arrived at school early every morning and didn't leave until 7:00, 8:00, 9:00, or 10:00 o'clock every evening. There were always practices, weight training classes, film review sessions, coaches meetings, booster club meetings, and countless other things to be done before I was able to leave. We lived thirty minutes away from school, and life for my son was very, very challenging. Clint would wait for me, hungry for dinner and stressed by assignments that he needed to do in the quiet of our home. He was an honors student who took as much pride in his academics as he did in football. He never complained but it broke my heart to see him get home late in the evening and do homework past midnight every day.

Clint graduated from high school just as his younger brother Mark arrived as a freshman. Mark had no interest in football. His loves were academics, volleyball, and theatre. He was also an honors student who would have hours of homework every night. It wouldn't be fair for him to make the same sacrifices that his brother did, and I knew that I was a father first and a coach second, so I retired from coaching. I became the water boy for the volleyball team and a stage-crew volunteer for theatre. It is a decision that I have never regretted, not even for a second.

Within a week after my announcement to leave coaching, our principal, Martin Plourde, asked me to do something that I really didn't want to do. He asked me to start a program at La Serna High School to help our most at-risk students. After so many years of film review, booster club meetings, coaching clinics, off-season weight training programs, fundraising, practice planning, game preparation, and seven-day work weeks, all I wanted to do was to relax and just teach writing and literature. I have always loved teaching as much or more than coaching, and I was looking forward to the time to prepare lessons that I never seemed to have time to prepare before. I wanted to simply be a teacher who didn't lead anything but my own classroom. My principal had something else in mind for me.

I received the greatest challenge of my professional career late in the game. I was asked to develop a program for students who had never known much success in school at all. I was told that these were students who were falling through the cracks and would not graduate high school if they did not receive immediate intervention. I initially resisted, but I had known Martin for twenty years, and he knew what buttons to push. We both have big soft spots in our hearts for kids who struggle, and he used my soft spot to convince me to start a new chapter in my professional life. I'm glad he did because his vision soon became my new obsession and led to the most gratifying, meaningful experience I have ever had as an educator.

My official title is teacher, but in reality, I am paid to be a father (or a grandpa) to teenagers I quickly come to love. I work with at-risk students who see no real value in education. My job is to turn them around, get them back on track and motivated. I realize that I can't do it with rigid curriculum and a ton of rules, so I use variety, passion, laughter, and games to get them pointed in the right direction. I show them that I care about them every day and I surround them with others who also care. My main goal is to give them a reason to try.

I recruit the finest students in our school to become academic mentors for these at-risk kids. These mentors tutor them in their assignments but more importantly, they listen to them and show them that they care. Days in my classroom are filled with sounds of mentors encouraging their reluctant students as they complete their assignments. There are "high fives" and big smiles when students show their mentors A's on their tests taken earlier that day. There are cookies, Cup-of-Noodles, and burritos, feeding hungry students as they work on assignments; and every day, there is hope, laughter, and a lot of love.

Growing up, I was like many of my current students. I had loving parents who cared but were lost in the circumstances of a very complicated world. They worked hard just to pay the mortgage and the grocery bills. They were not at all capable of recognizing the threats and dangers of our own neighborhood. Drugs, crime, and violence affected them much differently from the way that many parents are affected today. They were not direct victims. They did not take drugs, abuse their children, or spend time in prison. They were solid citizens who believed in all the right things. They simply didn't see the danger at their door until it was too late. They were just oblivious to the temptation of alcohol, drugs, and the gangster lifestyle until they had to bail my brother out of jail again and again. By then, it was too late. Drugs and a warped sense of values had my brother by the neck and wouldn't let go.

I can recall a constant sense of confusion and desperation in my home. My parents, despite their good hearts and best intentions, could not break the increasingly strong bonds that were dragging my brother toward a horrible life and were starting to grab me as well. Their prayers were beautiful and heartbreaking, but not effective. It was the clarity and strength of my coaches that anchored me. Their patient belief in me taught me the lessons I needed to survive and be successful. These are the same lessons I try to give to my students.

In our increasingly complex, disengaged, and superficial society, it is exactly what they need.

In working with my at-risk students, I am reminded of my own youth, of times that I came so close to listening to the wrong people and going down a different, dark path. What saved me were not the beautifully designed lessons given to me by outstanding teachers. Before embracing those lessons, I had to get myself right…from the inside out. No, what saved me were the teachers and coaches who reached deep into my soul to give me a sense of identity and a reason to try. These great people armed me with the core values that eventually directed my life. From them, I learned to look beyond the particular moment, day, or week in which I found myself. I came to realize the value of patience and the need for sacrifice to achieve my goals. The fact that I even created goals and worked toward them would never have been possible without the intervention of some amazing teachers and coaches.

I'm fortunate! I was once just like so many of my students. What literally saved me were my teachers and coaches who taught me the invaluable lessons of life. These lessons transcended all the challenges I faced as a student and person. These saviors were simply people with a clear vision and the unselfish, dedicated desire to share these lessons with me. They have made all the difference in my life. They taught my mind, developed my skills, but most importantly, they coached my soul.

While I was doing my student teaching years ago at Monte Vista High School in Whittier, something happened one afternoon that made an indelible impression on me as an educator, one that I think about every single day. On a late afternoon in the teacher's lounge, I was grading papers when John DeNoon, an assistant principal, walked into the room.

He and I were the only people in the lounge and he approached with a question, "What are you teaching?" I responded by telling him that I was teaching English, to which he repeated his question, "No. What are you teaching?" I thought for a second and in an attempt to clarify, I told him that I was teaching sophomore and junior English classes.

He simply repeated, "No. *What* are you teaching?" I was a bit confused, but I replied with a more specific answer, "I'm teaching composition and American literature." I was surprised and somewhat annoyed when he, once again, repeated his question, "No. *What* are you teaching?" I expressed my frustration at his question, elaborating on the specifics of my lessons and asking him what he meant by continuing to ask something that I felt I had adequately answered.

He calmly looked me in the eye and said, "No. You're teaching *kids*, and don't ever forget it." With that, he walked out of the room. The memory of that conversation has never left me; and every day, I remind myself of what he told me.

Many years after my encounter with Mr. DeNoon in the teacher's lounge that day, his message was made even more important and relevant to me. After my sons, Clint and Mark, each graduated from high school and UCLA, I used to enjoy talking with them about their experiences. I asked each of them who they felt was their best teacher. They mentioned several people who were dynamic and influential, but both of them singled out one teacher who they loved, respected, and enjoyed the most. Each of them identified Karen Lantz, their high school Advanced Placement English teacher as the best they ever had. When I asked them why she was so good, they said pretty much the same thing. Yes, she taught them and challenged them with great lessons, but the thing that set her apart was how she *treated* them. She made them feel smart, important, and confident. She listened to them with compassion and respect. This insight reinforces my own awareness of what I need to be as a teacher.

1

RESILIENCE

"I am not what happened to me.
I am what I choose to become."

~ Carl Jung

AMALIA AND TIMARI

Amalia entered my classroom as a sophomore. She had a 0.45 grade point average and had been chronically truant and defiant as a freshman. Her mentor could not have come from a more different world. Timari was an outstanding student from a stable home who had almost perfect attendance. Time, patience, and love bonded these two, and Amalia began coming to school every day. Her grades drastically improved, and she became a model student. On one Friday afternoon, Juanita Garza, our attendance coordinator, saw me in the office and began following me, saying that she had to tell me something. Well, with the students I teach, this is not usually good news for me, so I gritted my teeth and listened.

Surprisingly, she told me a wonderful story. Amalia stood in the attendance line that morning and when she got to the window, she said, "Mrs. Garza, you haven't called me in this year." Mrs. Garza told her that it was because she had been doing such a great job in coming to school every day. Then, Amalia asked, "Did you see my grades?" Mrs. Garza looked them up on the computer and screamed, "Oh my God!" Amalia had earned a 3.25 grade point average on her quarter grades. They both cried and hugged, but the story does not end there.

The next Monday morning, we all received an email from Rita Stevens, our assistant principal. On Saturday night, Amalia had been with her older brother whom she adored when four gang members approached with the deadly question, "Where you from?" Before Gabriel, her brother, could answer, shots were fired and he died in her arms. Amalia wept uncontrollably as her brother was taken away. She was lost. The person she loved and looked up to more than any-one else in the world was suddenly gone forever. She didn't know what to do or who to talk to as she stayed awake all night, reliving the horror of gunshots, blood, and death. She needed someone to help her and eventually decided to ask the person who had made such a difference in her life during the past few months.

On the morning after her brother's murder, the first person Amalia called for love and support was Timari, her academic men-tor, who took her out to breakfast. They talked for hours. Timari held Amalia's hand and cried with her for hours, trying to ease her incredible pain. The experience was so powerful for Timari that she wrote about it extensively in her college application essays. The enormity of the loss and the deeply moving experience of helping Amalia's recovery during the months that followed never dissipated, and Timari entered college the next year with the goal of becom-ing a school counselor. Her compassionate presence in Amalia's life strengthened the bond between them beyond anything either one of them ever thought possible, leading to a lifetime friendship.

It took a week before we could ensure Amalia's safety because she had witnessed a gang murder. She called my classroom several times, asking to come back. Those calls, in themselves, were amazing requests from someone who once hated school. Finally, she was able to return and passed all of her classes for the rest of the year. Amalia was rescued by Timari, someone who couldn't have possibly come from a more different place. Amalia was led through this terrible period in her life, holding the loving hand of an older friend who truly cared. It's strange but magical how circumstance can thrust people into situations that change their lives so profoundly.

2

TRUST

"To be trusted is a greater compliment than being loved."

~ George MacDonald

HUGO

Hugo was a sophomore with a mean streak and gang affiliation when he entered my class. His tall, lanky frame moved slowly and exuded anger and defiance. Early on, he would stare at me with contempt while I addressed the class. He would smile and talk with a select group of his friends, but never to me. It took a long time to break down the wall of his deeply entrenched hatred for anything that resembled authority. I had to humble myself by not taking offense to his defiance over a long period of time before he loosened up. Like his classmates, I fed him soup and cookies when he was hungry. I gave him cold water from the refrigerator I have in class when he was hot and thirsty. I also gave him space. We butted heads often, but he slowly grew to trust me.

During the many weeks of adjusting to each other's attitudes, he slowly began talking to me and even laughing with me over some silly thing that happened in class; yet, he still maintained his gangster image. He didn't want to appear weak or submissive around his friends, around anyone.

One day in class, he was wearing his baseball cap, which was forbidden in our school dress code policy. I asked him to take it off, and he refused. I asked him again, and he ignored me. We were at an impasse. I could yield to his refusal, but that would mean relinquishing control of my class, and I just could not let that happen. I asked him again to take off his cap. He looked up at me and smirked, so I simply grabbed the hat from his head and told him that he could pick it up after school. His immediate reaction was to snarl a threat, "Don't piss me off!"

He picked the wrong guy to threaten. I told him to step outside so we could discuss this. When we were outside the classroom, I looked him square in the eye and said, "What are you doing? When you're hungry, don't I feed you? When you're thirsty, don't I give you something to drink? You never have to worry about pencils, pens, paper, or anything else! I take care of you and treat you like a prince, and you treat me like a piece of garbage! What the hell!"

At that point, a student from inside the class stuck her head out the door and told me that there was a counselor on the phone who needed to talk to me. I told Hugo to wait right there until I got back. When I finished the phone call, I walked back outside the classroom. Hugo was in tears, sobbing. I asked him what was wrong, and he looked at me and said, "Nobody's ever talked to me like that before."

I told him that I guess I'm a weird and different guy but that I simply told him the truth. I told Hugo that I wasn't there to hurt him but to help him. I had to enforce a school rule because I'm loyal to my colleagues, but I am also loyal to him. I wasn't "taking" the hat from him permanently but was going to hold it for him until after school so that he wouldn't get in trouble for wearing it. He just looked at me with wet eyes and said, "Okay. I understand." I told him to gather himself and when he felt comfortable coming back into class, just come back in.

Hugo came back after school to retrieve his baseball cap. He even smiled and said thank you. I never had a problem with him after that. Years later after he graduated, I received an award at a school district ceremony. I was told to invite special people to share the moment with me. Hugo was one of the people I invited. When I parked my car and began walking to the school board room where the ceremony was to occur, I saw Hugo with two of his buddies and former students of mine whom I had invited. They were wearing dress shirts and ties, so I commented on how nice they looked. "You look pretty fucking good, too, Mr. LaVigne." I shook my head and smiled as we all walked into the room together.

While I was proctoring the CAHSEE (California High School Exit Exam) during Hugo's sophomore year, I noticed he was distracted and wasn't even trying. I asked another teacher to watch my area and I took Hugo outside. "What are you doing?" I asked, reminding him that this test was a very big deal. He told me that some guys from a nearby gang would be waiting for him after school to kill him.

"What's the difference? Why should I even try?" was his response.

I asked him if he trusted me. He said, "Yes," so I told him to take care of the test and I'd take care of everything else. I assured him that no one was going to hurt him. He went in and finished the test while I went to our dean who contacted local police who defused the threat. Hugo passed the CAHSEE and graduated on time. He went on to attend classes at Rio Hondo College while working as a security guard. He's no longer a gangster; he's a man with goals, hopes, and dreams.

3

PURPOSE

"The purpose of life is a life of purpose."

~ Robert Byrne

MY BROTHER BUTCH

"**P**unk!"

I stepped outside and heard a voice as I closed the back door. "Punk. Come here. Over here!"

I thought that maybe I was imagining that voice in the darkness of our backyard.

"Over here, stupid!"

The voice came from the far corner of our backyard, behind the block wall and next to the telephone pole. It was Butch, my older brother. It was Halloween night, and I was more than a little bit scared and upset *without* hearing any voices. My brother hadn't been home in two days and my parents were all kinds of things.... angry, scared, sad, and desperate. I was eight-years-old and I don't think I knew what the word desperate meant, but I understood the

19

feeling by the look in my parent's eyes as they worried about where my brother was.

"Hurry up. Over here! Get your ass over here."

I followed the voice and edged my way to my brother's head sticking out from behind the wall.

"Whatta ya want? Where you been? Mom and Dad are mad!"

As I got closer, I could see Butch's face…mainly his eyes. It was dusk, but I could plainly see his eyes had that bloodshot, watery look that I didn't understand back then. I knew it wasn't good, because every time his eyes looked like that, I got my butt kicked. Something bad always happened when his eyes looked like that.

"Shhh. Don't talk so loud. I need some money. Go inside and get the money in Dad's wallet. Don't let him see you.

"That's not your money. I'm not gonna steal from Dad. I'm gonna tell." Dad kept his wallet on his dresser. It was always there, but to touch his wallet, let alone take money from it, was more than I could even think of. I didn't. I ran inside and yelled as loud as I could, "Butch is outside!"

Mom and Dad ran to the back door. Dad threw it open and looked across the yard as Smoky, our dog, jumped and ran around as though we were there to play. My father's eyes swept the block wall that separated our yard from our neighbor's, and looked for what seemed like hours. After finally giving up, he looked at Mom with an expression I will never forget. His face was sad and angry at the same time. It was also scared, unsure. My mom started crying, and we all went back inside the house.

That was the real start of it. Butch had been in trouble before but nothing like this. He was gone for days until the police called in the middle of one night. Butch was in jail, a juvenile detention center in Stockton. He and Ted, his friend, had jumped a railway car and ended up in Northern California where they stole a car and wrecked it. They were drunk. Dad got up and drove all night to get him out of jail. He went to work the next day - late, but he got there anyway. Dad didn't have paid days off, and we couldn't afford to lose a whole day's pay.

Butch never seemed grateful or happy about being home. All I remember is him being angry, running away from home several times, and each time, my parents would worry, cry, wait, and pray. I said the same prayer for over ten years every night, but Butch kept getting into trouble. He cut school, ran away, stole cars, broke into stores, got drunk, and took drugs. He got locked up more than once, and I vividly remember going to see him in jail. My mom's face was always sad, but hopeful, and my dad's face, ashamed and increasingly resentful. My brother seemed to be on a mission to destroy our family, to break our parents' hearts.

On that first night he ran away, I remember thinking I had to do something to make up for what he did, what he was. As the years went by, that feeling grew and I had to make my parents know that one of their sons was not a bum. I had to be the one to make them proud and happy. That feeling motivated me in everything I did for many years. When I started playing football, I found out that I was pretty good. School also came easy for me. Somewhere along the way, I decided that these two things, football and school, could erase the sadness and disappointment in my parents' eyes. I attacked each one with as much effort and drive that I could give. From that point on, my life had purpose, a goal and a reason to try. All I needed was help.

For many years, my brother took every opportunity to slap, kick, punch, and hurt me. His taunts and bullying continued through my high school years, but I found football and saw it as an escape from my personal hell at home. That escape saved me because it led me to great men, my coaches, who changed my life.

4

FAITH

*"Death is no more than passing
from one room into another.
But there's a difference for me, you know.
Because in that other room,
I shall be able to see."*

~ Helen Keller

JAVIER

While teaching and coaching at Santa Fe High School, life's cruel reality hit me square in the face with a force that brought me to my knees.

The funeral was the hardest part. I went to the Rosary a few days before and stood in the back of the church overflowing with Javier's family, friends, and teammates. I listened to the voices as I prayed with them, "Our Father, Who art in Heaven, hallowed be Thy name. Thy kingdom come...," seamlessly followed by repetitions of, "Hail Mary, full of grace, The Lord is with thee, blessed art thou amongst women and blessed is the fruit of thy womb, Jesus…." The weeping mixed with the prayers made the unthinkable real. I was lost in the sadness, but didn't feel the full impact of the tragedy until I stood next to his grave.

Javier was one of my football players, a uniquely dynamic kid who set himself apart in many ways. He and his family moved to our area just two years earlier, leaving a gang-infested neighborhood in Huntington Park for a new beginning in Norwalk where he could start fresh. He had a kind disposition that was seen as more of a weakness than it was a strength in his former neighborhood. Kindness is not as valuable as toughness in those areas. He was fairly short at about 5' 7" but weighed over 260 pounds. Easily the strongest kid I ever coached, he could bench press over 400 pounds. On the field, he was a terror. Freakishly quick for his size and incredibly aggressive, he soon earned a starting position on our defensive line and became the most feared player our opponents faced. He endeared himself to all of our players and coaches with his engaging, playful attitude that he maintained even as he mauled every teammate and opposing player he faced. Considered invincible by everyone on our team, his death was difficult to accept by those who knew him.

Javier went to the Uptown Whittier Festival with two of his friends and teammates. He had given up his gang affiliation but continued to dress like a gangster, not quite making the complete transformation from his former life. He and his friends had just gotten into a car with Javier sitting in the driver's seat. His friend, Franco, was seated next to him in the front seat. As Javier started the car, Franco saw the shiny barrel of a pistol that suddenly appeared next to his head. He reacted by leaning forward to avoid the shot but was hit anyway. The bullet traveled through his shoulder, finding its final destination in Javier's heart. It all happened so quickly, giving Javier only a few seconds to react. He stepped on the gas pedal and drove over the curb before the car smashed into a tree about twenty yards ahead of them. Javier didn't move as he slumped over the steering wheel.

The police later determined that the shooting was a gang initiation. Javier, Franco, and Justin became targets because they were dressed like gangsters who were not from the area. Javier and Franco were both rushed to the hospital where Franco was saved. Unfortunately, Javier was not. In an instant, his family's dream of a new life with a new beginning was destroyed in a senseless act of violence they tried so hard to avoid. Days later, we all stood by the casket of this indestructible kid who had so much to live for.

The priest's words were drowned out by the wailing of Javier's mother, "Mijo! Oh, Mijo!" Placing roses on the casket as we slowly walked past, we heard the pitiful, gut-wrenching cries of a mother's disbelief, "No, God! Please! Not my son! No! No! God, please!" She continued with only the pain a mother can feel as Javier's casket was moved before being lowered into the grave. She clutched and scratched the top of the casket and begged for it not to be true, but it was. Her precious son, the baby she held when he was an infant, the little boy that made her laugh with his precocious antics, was now gone, and she was inconsolable.

The shocked, empty faces of everyone there made me feel lost and powerless. I had no words of comfort or wisdom to share with my players as they shuffled from the grave. There was a constant sound of crying and hushed voices that struggled to offer support and comfort to his weeping family. In the days and weeks that followed, Javier's friends would stop by my classroom and come to visit me at my home, looking for some answer I could not give.

"Coach, if this happened to Javier, it could happen to anyone, to me! He was the strongest guy on our team, and now he's dead. I don't understand." They all had the same emotionally charged questions about their own mortality. Javier had been so fearless and powerful, but it didn't help him. He was taken in a random, stupid act of cowardly bravado, leaving everyone around him keenly aware of the danger of simply being in the wrong place at the wrong time. I had no answers that could bring him back or calm the fears of his young friends.

Javier didn't deserve to die. His only mistake was wearing clothes that identified him with the same gangster life he had worked so hard to escape. His choice not to dress like that was just a final step in his development. I knew this step would come in time, but time ran out. He had taken so many strides to build a better life: earning good grades, acting like the leader he was born to be, and letting down his guard to get along with others. Dammit, he was so close!

Having a distorted sense of values when he first arrived on campus, Javier struggled early. Time and patience made him understand that there were principles that could guide him and make his life better. Sudden outbursts of anger and a deep distrust of others slowly melted away through repeated talks with his coaches and forced sessions of conflict resolution. Javier's better grades and behavior were simply by-products of our attempts to reach his heart. Like almost every kid I have ever taught or coached, he grew to like the feeling of accountability while enjoying this new sense of belonging. As his teachers and coaches, it was up to us to teach him more about life than about football, math, or history. We came close but didn't finish the job.

Standing next to Javier's grave, I was incapable of saying anything that would stop the heartache of his grieving parents or calm the minds of his devastated friends. What was clear was the realization that teaching and coaching is a lot more than I had ever imagined. It's powerful; yet, it can render you powerless. All I knew at that moment was that I wanted and needed to do more. I just didn't know how.

In the weeks and months that followed, the hurt of this senseless act remained strong. I struggled to find some reason for this happening and was finally stripped of what is Earthly as I reached deep into my faith to find some sort of good that could come from something so wrong. On my own, I could never understand the why, but through my faith in God, I found some peace in giving in to the Almighty's omniscient plan.

When the tragedy of unexpected death strikes and confusion and pain overwhelm reason, I have always had to decide how to provide comfort to my students and football players by asking a question: "Are you a person of faith?" If the answer is no, then I simply say that it is impossible to understand, but we have to live a life that will bring honor to his name. When the answer is yes, I say what I told so many of Javier's friends and teammates. Javier is definitely with God now and at peace. He loves us and doesn't want us to be sad or to give up or become bitter. He wants us to celebrate and honor his life by living ours with respect and compassion. I encourage these heartbroken souls to reach out to God and live so that someday, we can see Javier again in Heaven.

That's what I believe and that's what I say. I still talk to Javier as well as to God, asking for the wisdom and strength to keep going. My life would be empty without that faith.

5

IDENTITY

"Nothing of me is original.
I am the combined effort
of everyone I've ever known."

~ Chuck Palahniuk

COACH TORRES

I entered junior high school with the confidence that I could make the flag football team. I did, and it was there that I came to know my first really memorable coach, Dick Torres. He was our physical education teacher as well as our coach. He was an impressive man for many reasons. He was in his thirties and looked exactly like a coach should. He was strong, had hairy arms, and always seemed confident. There was nothing that I thought he couldn't do. He was also funny. He wasn't afraid to laugh with us, and it was obvious that he liked and believed in us. That wasn't always easy because we weren't very good as a football team, but that didn't seem to be important to him. He was competitive, but what he cared about most was for us to always try and to behave like "nice young men".

When football season was done, Coach Torres encouraged us to go out for basketball in the winter and track in the spring. He taught us to play, but more importantly, he showed us how to have fun as athletes. In his own kind and nurturing way, he made us see ourselves as students, athletes, and gentlemen. He knew every one of us and always praised and encouraged all "his boys". To this day, he is the most positive, nurturing person I have ever known. What made him even more special was his patience and sense of humor. It wasn't uncommon for him to sit with us individually or in a group and just talk and listen to us.

We had fun with him, locking him in the locker room by placing benches or rolling a car in front of the door. At times, we even hid his car from him, getting inside, releasing the parking brake, putting it in neutral, and pushing it to a place out of sight. He acted agitated, but we always noticed him shaking his head and smiling as he looked for his car or pushed barriers away from the locker room doors. Sometimes after we had done something especially childish, he would look for us in the locker room as he yelled, "Where are you termites? You're in deep trouble!" But we always knew that the trouble would be short-lived and soon enough, he would go back to being his positive, friendly self. He was a lot of fun.

I didn't realize it then, but besides my father, he was my first real role model. I liked everything about him and thought, "Wouldn't it be great to be like Coach Torres?" Little did I know then that one day, I would get my chance.

We kept in contact through the years and became especially close during the last ten years of his life. I don't think that two weeks ever went by without me calling him or him calling me. We'd talk and laugh; and every time we spoke, I felt like a million bucks when I hung up the phone. His gift of happiness was shared often, providing us all with feelings of love and confidence. These feelings were close to absent in my own home, and to find them in a teacher and coach made an indelible impression on me.

I was glad that he got to spend one final day with some of his boys at a get-together for about thirty of us and our wives at a park less than a year before he passed away. He spent the afternoon laughing and sharing stories with everyone. He was in Heaven! When people started to leave, I asked him if he would like to join some of us for a traditional cigar and drink to end the evening. He was excited, so with him sitting shotgun, I drove his truck to our friend's house where several of us sat in the backyard with a cigar in one hand and a beverage in the other. He chose not to smoke but absolutely loved the whole experience. He sat with all the wives like a big, proud rooster holding court.

During our regular telephone conversations, he would always ask me about what I was doing. He loved to hear about our program for at-risk students and the stories of kids whose lives had been changed by it. He loved everything that was good for young people. He was also amazingly nurturing and reassuring. He made me proud to be a teacher and coach. Just as he did when I was younger, he reaffirmed my sense of self-worth and identity. He delighted in hearing about every little thing that we were doing in the classroom.

Within six months of our gathering at the park with so many of his former students, he was gone. We were all devastated. Less than a year after his death, I received a call, notifying me that I was selected California State Teacher of the Year. When I was informed, I couldn't get Dick Torres out of my mind.

He used to tell me all the time, "Ken LaVigne, you are amazing! You are incredible! Someday, you're gonna be on Oprah! Someday, you're gonna be Teacher of the Year, and we'll raise our glasses and celebrate together!" His genuine enthusiasm warmed my heart, and his words were etched into my brain. I would have given anything to have shared that honor and recognition with him in person. I feel good, though, because my faith lets me know that he was watching it all from a much higher, better seat. I hope he knows how much I miss him. I think of him and talk to him almost every single day. I sure hope he's listening. I believe that he is!

I learned a lot from Coach Torres. I learned to believe in myself and to have fun in what I did. He taught me that my behavior as a young man was far more important than winning a game or scoring points. His honest enthusiasm about life and his unlimited belief in us as people motivated and inspired me, giving me a template on how to treat my own students and athletes when I became a teacher and a coach. He was a great educator in every sense of the word because he demonstrated the powerful impact that caring leadership can have on young minds and spirits, something I constantly think about when I stand in front of teenagers who need that same encouraging mentor.

6

LISTENING

*"Too often, we underestimate the power
of a touch, a smile, a kind word,
a listening ear, an honest compliment,
or the smallest act of caring,
all of which have the potential
to turn a life around."*

~ Leo Buscaglia

TREVAUN

My first real job as both a teacher and coach was at a Catholic high school. I was also asked to be the dean of discipline. During my first week on the job, I was sitting in my office as Dean of Discipline one morning when a young man, a sophomore student, was sent to me with a note from a strict and rigid nun I would later come to know well. She listed the behavioral infractions of this student as though they had been high treason, but they seemed pretty minor to me. What was immediately obvious, however, was the anger and rage in this kid's eyes. The look in his eyes coupled with the fact that he was a good-sized, muscular kid for a sophomore made him seem a bit ominous. I decided to do something I learned in my education classes called responsive listening. I felt that this was a good time for it so I welcomed this young man into my office, shut the door, sat down behind my desk, and said, "You seem very angry. I'd like to hear why." That's all it took to cut this kid loose.

First of all, I believe that everyone sees things from a totally unique perspective, a seat from which to view the world that is determined by his/her genetic composition as well as all of the experiences in his/her life. That being said, this kid could not have been sitting in a more different seat than me. He was African American and his name was Trevaun. I closed the door to my office, sat, and listened.

Trevaun lived with both parents in a very dangerous, gang-infested area. He had four older brothers. One of Trevaun's brothers was on a full football scholarship at a major university. Another one was said to be serving a life sentence for murder. His parents sent him to a private parochial school to get him away from the constant threat of danger in his neighborhood. This is who confronted me in my office, and I can see his face in my mind today just as I saw it so many years before.

Trevaun grabbed the edge of my desk with both hands and started yelling at me as the veins in his neck and arms bulged. He gritted his teeth and spit out hatred and anger, calling me a "fat, white son of a bitch" among many other things. His tirade had more cursing in it than anything I had ever heard before. That is saying a lot because as a football player and coach, I heard more than my share of cuss words. He came out with some words and phrases that were really good ones that I had never heard before, so I said a few times, "Hold on, man. I gotta write that down. That was a good one!" He was so angry, hateful, and bitter! He just went on and on for nearly twenty minutes while I practiced strategies I had been taught, listening strategies. I was trying to be a pure, nonjudgmental listener, and it was a wild ride.

After about twenty minutes of screaming and cussing at me, Trevaun became very emotional for about fifteen to twenty minutes, telling me about the frustration and desperation that he and his family members had experienced over the years. He spoke much more quietly then, but the pain and sadness seemed to spew out of him as his heart and spirit convulsed within him. It was a powerful thing to see. When Trevaun finished speaking emotionally, he seemed visibly better. I began interjecting a bit more in our conversation, asking his hobbies, likes, dislikes, etc. That lasted for another fifteen to twenty minutes, and when Trevaun left my office, I was totally exhausted and I bet he was, too.

Because Trevaun had violated a couple school rules (I think he was not wearing a belt and talked back to his teacher, the nun) and because I was the dean, I had to call his mother and suspend him for a couple days. I explained this to him as well as to his mom, and they understood. Finally, I emerged from my office with Trevaun. I handed him his suspension papers and he gave me a big hug before leaving to meet his mother outside.

Now, all the offices and classrooms were indoors at this school, and my office was smack dab in the middle, directly across the hallway from the principal's office, curriculum office, and business office as they all intersected. Checking Trevaun's student file after we talked, I learned that he had quite an extensive list of offenses at the school....even though he was just beginning his sophomore year. After walking back into my office after I suspended him, I learned that he also had a big reputation as well. As soon as I sat in my chair, several secretaries crowded into my office, chirpy as hell. They were completely flabbergasted that Trevaun hugged me before leaving for his suspension. They had all heard the sounds of yelling in my office, and I assume they thought much, if not most, of it was from me. They all looked at me with this wondrous stare. One of the ladies said, "What did you do? Did you hit him?" I smiled at her and said, "Of course not!"

"Then what did you do? You must have done something!"

"Yes. I did do something," I replied. "I **listened** to him. Honest! It is as simple as that."

I don't think they believed me. I think they felt that I did something sinister or made a secret threat that would certainly make him think twice. The truth is that if I had threatened or berated Trevaun, he would have left my office even more bitter and enraged than he was when he entered. No. The truth was that Trevaun and I made a connection simply because I respected him enough to listen to him and value his words. I did learn quite a lot about him that day and during the weeks and months that followed.

Trevaun and his brothers were all very athletic. They were smart, too. The oldest brothers had found more than their share of trouble in their local public school, so his mother, the matriarch of the family, and her husband worked hard to make enough money to send their younger sons to a private Catholic high school out of their community. Trevaun's mother was a teacher herself, but was overwhelmed by the sheer scope of dangers and temptations in her own community. She had a big heart and loved her family very much. Trevaun had played football at our school the previous year, earning the Most Valuable Player award on the freshman team in the process. However, he was a "hot head" and did not get along with his coaches at all. He barely got along with most of his teammates. Although he was witty, genuine, and generally friendly, he also had a short fuse that could be easily lit at any moment. He decided not to play his sophomore year and maybe never play again. Because I got to know him after our players had already completed required summer weight training and conditioning plus weeks of practice, it wasn't possible for him to play football that year even if he had a change of heart. That change of heart finally came.

Throughout the fall and winter months, I made it a point to know where Trevaun was on campus at any given time. I'd make sure to make my way there during morning break and lunch. I got to know him better and better, and he seemed more and more at ease talking with me. It wasn't all serious talk, either. We'd joke around, laugh, and share little stories about everyday things. I could tell that

Trevaun trusted me just as I respected and trusted him. After the head coach who brought me to this school abruptly left, the principal and players asked me not to leave. I knew that I wasn't ready to be a head coach, especially at a school with a very low enrollment and an extremely challenging schedule, but I decided to stay because of the kids, not the principal. It didn't take long for the word to get out about me becoming the new head coach.

A few days after agreeing to stay on, I saw Trevaun on campus during lunchtime. "Hey. I hear that you're gonna be head coach. Is that right?"

"That's what's happening, Trevaun. How do you feel about that?"

"I think I want to play football now if you're the head coach. You okay with that?"

"I'm happy to hear that! I'll be proud to be your coach. I need you to know something, though. There will probably be times that you'll hate my guts because I have to push you guys hard. You gotta trust me and know that whatever I do, I'm doing it for the best....for you and all the players. Does that sound reasonable?"

"Hell yeah! I'm ready to go. Let's get started."

Trevaun went out for football that next year and was one of our real stars, earning first team All-League and All-Southeast Area as a cornerback. He had seven interceptions and a ton of big plays, making him a highly recruited player after his junior season. There were several colleges that were very interested in him. His grades improved and everything was looking great, and then it happened.

I was called into our principal's office on a spring afternoon during Trevaun's junior year. Our principal told me that he had to expel Trevaun for severe disrespect and defiance. Since Trevaun had so many incidents during his freshman year, the principal told me that he had no other choice. I was incredulous and impassioned in my request for Father to reconsider. "What about all the progress Trevaun's made in the past year? Look at his grades! Look at his behavior compared to where he was just a year ago! What did he do, anyway?"

I was told that two teachers had confronted Trevaun at lunch that day and told him to go to the office for saying a few cuss words. I guess Trevaun wasn't moving fast enough, so one of the teachers grabbed his arm and started pushing and pulling him to the office. Trevaun obviously did not react well to this and told the teacher to get her damned hands off him. He said a few other choice words and then stormed away. The two teachers went directly to the principal and demanded that Trevaun be expelled. It was either "him or them", they supposedly said.

That was an easy choice from my perspective. Should we keep a kid who grew up in a true ghetto and had overcome crime, drugs, and violence to earn good grades, drastically improve his behavior, and excel on the athletic field or should we keep two teachers who were so petty and insecure that they likely purposefully pushed this kid to his limits as retaliation for things done in the past? It seemed simple to me. It was the teachers who acted immaturely and without perspective. It was the teachers who delivered the ultimatum: "It's either him or us." I said that it was a "no-brainer". Get rid of the teachers! Heck, that wasn't even necessary. Give it some time and let cooler heads prevail. Sure, Trevaun deserved consequences for his disrespect and defiance, but if his actions were viewed in the totality of his circumstances with consideration for how far he had come, there is no way that a school, principal, or teacher could throw a kid like that away. We were his only hope. I literally got down on my knees and begged Father Hill, the principal, not to expel Trevaun, but he decided to do it anyway. I was deeply, deeply sad … and disillusioned.

It was incredibly difficult seeing Trevaun go. I spoke to his mother and we cried together and promised to pray for each other. She still wanted to keep him away from all the dangers and temptations of their neighborhood, so she enrolled him into a small Christian school. He played football during the fall of his senior year, but the small schools like the one he was attending did not have regular eleven-man football. They played a variation of the game, "eight man football", that was wide open and wild. It was a fun game to watch but eight-man football did not garner much interest from college coaches. Trevaun played well his senior season and I think he scored over 50 touchdowns in that pass-happy, semi-flag-football they were playing. I still tried to point coaches in his direction, but his expulsion was one too many things to overcome. Trevaun did not get that scholarship that he had worked so hard for.

On the night of our football awards banquet, we had our gymnasium filled with hundreds of players, parents, cheerleaders, faculty, and friends. As I approached the podium at the front of the gym to begin our awards program, I looked at the very back of the gym and saw a young man, standing between the double doors gesturing for me to come to where he was. I stepped away from the microphone and stared at him as I said, "Trevaun?" That only made him motion to me in bigger, quicker strokes, asking for me to go toward him. I took a step to my side so that I was behind the podium and microphone. I spoke clearly and loudly as I said into the microphone, "Trevaun, please come up here. You belong here. Please come on up."

Then I saw this tall, athletic young man walk right down the center aisle of the gymnasium. He was carrying two things. One was a sort of a combination pillow and stuffed animal. It was a bear, and his mother had made it for me. She used to call me her teddy bear for watching over her son. The second thing that Trevaun was carrying was a plaque with some beautiful words from him to me. After giving me these two things, he gave me a big hug and said, "I love you, Coach." I was overcome with emotion. "I love you, too, Trevaun."

It struck me that this tough, angry, black kid would let down his guard to hug his goofy white coach and allow himself to cry simply because I chose to listen to him one day. That simple act of listening led to a bond built from respect and compassion and continues to be a powerful lesson for me as well as for my students.

There is a side-note. I have often wondered what became of Trevaun. Many times, I've checked on the internet or asked people who might know, "Where's Trevaun and what's he doing now?" To be honest, I've always stopped short because I'm afraid to know for sure. I've heard a few times that things never worked out for him and he's serving a long prison sentence. That could all be nonsense, but the fact is that I am afraid to find out. It would be just too sad to know that he could have done some great things but didn't because he was blindsided by the worst in people who could have brought out the best in him. It would just be cool if he knew that I talk about him…with respect…every year to my students when I give them the huge lesson about the power of listening.

7

UNITY

"We are only as strong as we are united,
as weak as we are divided."

~ J.K. Rowling

SENIOR STUDENTS

My first job as a varsity football head coach was at a Catholic high school. During my first year, I was given the "plum" job of PE teacher. I was grateful but soon bored. I missed the interaction of the classroom, so I requested to go back. Although my degree and credential were in English, I was asked to teach religion. As a practicing Catholic, our principal thought it was a good idea for me to teach religion, so he assigned me to five classes of senior religion. I would be teaching every senior in the school, and it turned out to be a blessing of the highest order.

As a religion teacher, I wanted to make our lessons relevant and meaningful. Teaching New Testament Scripture gave me many opportunities to do this. One of my favorite memories from this period occurred while I was teaching St. Paul's epistles one year. In class, we discussed the format that St. Paul would use to write his epistles (or letters) to different Christian communities. He would initially greet them and compliment them on what they had been doing. Then, he would deliver his real message, the essence of each epistle. As we discussed different examples from the New Testament, it occurred to me that I had a very unique situation and opportunity that I shouldn't waste. I had every single senior in the school in one of my classes throughout the day, and it would be cool to give them a voice and platform, so I asked each of my senior classes a question, "What is something that you feel needs to be addressed to everyone at our school?"

We had great discussions in each class regarding the idea that they wanted to convey and the method of delivery. The seniors decided that their message should be a call for unity within the school. There had been various factions and incidents throughout the past year that led to bickering, arguing, and a splintering of what had always been an extremely close-knit student body. Each class discussed what they felt should be included in this letter and selected a couple class representatives who would meet with other class representatives to iron out the final product, a letter to the entire school community. They wrote a single-page, beautiful letter to every student, teacher, and staff member in our school, expressing their feelings and message. It was especially gratifying to me, as their teacher, that they used the basic format used by St. Paul in his epistles. What was most impressive, though, was the response elicited by their letter.

After composing this "epistle" to their classmates, the seniors had it photocopied on colored paper and met a couple hours before school one day to distribute the letters. All of our classes and student lockers were inside the walls of the school, which made it easy to get this done without being detected. At 6:00 AM, I opened the doors of our school to every member of the entire senior class who carefully inserted these letters through the vents of every locker in the school and on the desk of every teacher, secretary, counselor, and administrator. Their letter called for an "open sign of unity within the school" on that day only. The symbol of this unity would be a "High-Five in the Hallway" to remind everyone how important it was, despite our differences, to respect everyone else and hold tight to the beautiful and unique bond that we shared. These seniors asked that, in an open show of unity, we all "high-five" each other between classes throughout the day.

When the maintenance staff arrived at their normal time in the morning to open the school, they were surprised to see all the seniors already in the building. I explained what was going on and encouraged them to read the letter, which had also been given to them. Then the teachers, secretaries, and students began arriving. It was great fun to perform the clandestine task of watching students open their lockers and slowly read the letter, looking at each other with puzzled yet serious expressions. It was also interesting to see secretaries staring at the letters that were placed conspicuously on their desks as teachers slowly stepped out of their classrooms with letters in hand. Suspense was building! What would everyone do?

When the bell rang to signal it was time to go to first period class, the seniors did a fantastic job, high-fiving each other as well as their younger classmates as they passed each other in the hallway. Younger students initially looked tentative and a bit confused but quickly got into the spirit. In each of my classes during the day, we talked about not letting the momentum slow down and making every high-fiving passing period better than the previous one. The result was one of the most beautiful things I have ever seen in a school. Every student greeted classmates with a big smile and a high-five, and soon, teachers and secretaries stepped out of their rooms to join in the fun. Our principal stood on the main floor in the middle of the school and became the apex of that high-fiving enthusiasm. It was an awesome sight! At the end of the day, our student body president, one of our seniors, got on the school intercom and thanked everyone for their participation, reminding us all of the need for unity. The rest of the school year was dramatically different and better because of what these seniors did.

8

COMPASSION

"Compassion is not a relationship between the healer and the wounded. It's a relationship between equals. Only when we know our own darkness well can we be present with the darkness of others. Compassion becomes real when we recognize our shared humanity."

~ Pema Chödrön

VISITING PATIENTS

A djacent to the school where I taught and coached, there was a convalescent hospital and assisted living facility. I was teaching religion classes to every senior in our school and wanted to make our students' faith come alive through their actions of love and compassion. I decided to visit the facility and see if there was something we could do to help patients on a regular basis. I learned that, although there were some younger, disabled residents, most of the people who lived there were elderly and had no other place to go. Most of them rarely, if ever, had visitors. I had a brainstorm.

There were five days in a week and I had five religion classes. I cleared it with the administrator in charge, and began taking a different class to visit the patients every day of the week. Monday was first period. Tuesday was second period and so on. It took only a couple of minutes to walk to the facility from my classroom, and this offered the perfect opportunity for our students to put their faith to work, helping others. It really turned out to be a great thing for everyone. My students learned the true meaning of patience and compassion by serving the residents. They would read to them, talk and listen to them, laugh with them, play the piano, brush their hair, and take them outside for walks, pushing their wheelchairs as they chatted back and forth while surrounded by birds chirping and flowers dotting their stroll up and down the sidewalk between the school and their home. The residents just ate it up! It was a beautiful thing to see.

Through the years, I grew close to many of the residents who lived in the facility. There was Carol, a Chinese lady who was probably in her late 30's to mid 40's. She had obviously suffered from a very serious accident that severely limited the use of half of her body. I never heard her speak but she would always try, and sounds would come from her mouth as she held my hand across the table and smiled at me constantly. She was such a sweet person who just wanted and needed company.

Vince was a sweet, elderly man confined to a wheelchair. He was hearing-impaired and would try to have conversations with me even though he probably heard and understood about ten percent of what I said. We would sit inside in the recreation room or on warm days, we would sit in the garden. Vince would smile a lot and repeat the same phrases over and over while looking directly at me with the kindest face that reminded me of an elderly angel. His eyes would get big as he watched the hummingbirds dart from flower to flower in the lattice above our heads in the patio area. He just loved company.

Our football team used to run a fireworks stand in our school parking lot every year. There were always long hours of manning the booth to sell fireworks, and we had to spend nights parked next to the stand to protect it, but it helped us raise some much needed funds for equipment and uniforms. I used to set aside a large fireworks assortment well before July 4th each year. On the 4th, I would sneak out for an hour or two when it got dark and have a fireworks display for the residents of the convalescent home/assisted living facility. All the residents were like little kids and would just "Ooh!" and "Ahh!" with big eyes and bigger smiles. They were very special to me.

When I decided to leave this school for another job, I was asked by our principal to give a speech at graduation. We had our own football stadium and it was adjacent to the assisted living facility, and when I stepped up to the podium on stage, I saw something that made me stop in my tracks. The nurses and staff workers brought all of the residents outside and had seats for them along the chain link fence that separated their facility and our football field. Someone made a huge sign on butcher paper and taped it along the bottom of the fence just below their faces. In thick red paint it said, "We love you, Coach." It took everything in me to not get overly emotional and teary-eyed. They all cheered loudly when I was introduced. As I settled in at the podium, I looked over to them and said, "Thank you and I love you, too …….very much!" That is honestly one of the greatest moments in my life.

9

GRIT

"Grit is passion and perseverance
for very long-term goals. Grit is having stamina.
Grit is sticking with your future day in, day out,
not just for a week, not just for a month,
but for years, and working really hard
to make that future a reality.
Grit is living life like it's a marathon, not a sprint."

~ Angela Duckworth

COACH MAHLSTEDE

Other than my father, the man who had the most powerful impact on my life is Jack Mahlstede, my high school football coach. Sometimes, what we see on the outside of a person does not reveal the true depth and scope of their character. This is certainly the case with Jack Mahlstede. He was exactly the right person to come into my life at the exact time I needed him the most. When I met him, I was inconsistent. Sometimes I would be good and other times

I would be bad. I was on the hunt, exacting periodic revenge on guys who had beaten me up in my neighborhood when I was younger.... and weaker. I cared but I didn't care. I was really confused.

I met Coach Mahlstede during the summer before my sophomore year of high school. I had lost a ton of weight during my freshmen year; I wasn't a fat kid anymore. I was a 160-pound center who had been given a position on the varsity team instead of playing for junior varsity. As a member of the varsity team, I was told to attend a meeting in August at a restaurant where we would meet with our varsity head coach, Ed Mitchell, and be introduced to our new line coach, Jack Mahlstede. I looked forward to the meeting, mostly because we would eat at a restaurant. My family didn't go to restaurants very often, and the idea of eating at a place where you could have whatever you wanted and go back for seconds as many times as you liked was exciting. Those were my thoughts before that meeting, but it wasn't the food that made an impression on me that afternoon.

After we ate, Coach Mitchell, our head coach, got up and said a few things about the upcoming season. Coach Mitchell was a good coach and a nice man. He had also been an excellent football player in high school and college, playing at Arizona State as a running back. As a coach, he always said the right things. He was a gentleman with a good heart and talked to us about teamwork, dedication, and representing our school with honor. It was a really nice talk. When he was done, he introduced Coach Mahlstede.

Coach Mahlstede stood up and, boy, did he look mean! He was big and tanned with a crew cut so short that it almost seemed his head was shaved. His bald head and dark skin made him look like an oversized genie. He had a voice that sounded like he was swallowing sand while he was talking. He waited for a few seconds before speaking and had a scary half-smile on his face. Finally, he spoke, "All that Coach Mitchell said was great, but he left one important thing out. We're gonna kick some ASS! Just remember that! That's what football is all about. We're gonna kick some ass!" Then he sat down. We all sort of looked down at the table and turned our heads just a little to see each other's reaction. Everybody reacted pretty much the same. We were shocked…and intrigued.

The meeting ended shortly after Coach Mahlstede's talk, and we went home. On the way home and in the subsequent days before practice began, we all had the same anxiety and curiosity. What was going to happen? What kind of madman did they hire to coach us? We soon found out who he was as a coach on the field. In the years that followed, we learned much more about this complex man who had even more to give us off the field and in our lives.

When Hell Week started, we learned what Coach Mahlstede was all about. He moved and spoke at a faster pace than anyone I had ever seen or heard. He was all about effort, aggression, and accountability. To say that he was intense might be a bit of an understatement. He yelled and barked at every drill. It seemed that his eyes were everywhere, that he didn't miss anything. He was a technician and was obsessed about the smallest details. "You stepped with the wrong foot first! No! No! Don't look down! Keep your eyes up! Don't step to where the linebacker IS, step to where he's GOING! You stopped your feet after you made contact! That's bullshit! Block THROUGH the man! Don't over stride! You're out of control! Take short, deliberate steps!" Every comment he made was an exclamation. Nothing he said on the field was casual or without emotion. We learned pretty quickly that he would not tolerate us making the same mistake twice.

"Mental mistake! We can't afford mental mistakes! Get out of there! Give me somebody who WANTS to play!" He simply never let up.

Coach Mahlstede wasn't always negative. He was quick to praise you if you did well. He seemed especially excited when he saw a player give a second effort. "Great block! You kicked his ASS! Nice job of getting your hips involved in that block! Nice angle on that backer! Look at that effort! Son, you're gonna be an all-leaguer!" The clarity of his words and the intensity in his voice gave us all a clear understanding of what it would take for us to be successful. His personality dominated our team and after my sophomore season, Jack Mahlstede took over as head coach.

During the summer before my junior year, my friends and I learned something else about Coach Mahlstede. He liked to body surf and he took Billie, his wife, and Jeff and Kenny, his two young sons, to the same place we went to body surf, Lifeguard Station #3 next to the Huntington Beach Pier. We learned, though, that he had a whole new way of body surfing.

The first time he saw us at the beach, we were on our way to the water. We sat by the fire pits where all the girls were. He stationed himself and his family on the sand next to the water. When he saw us walking with our fins past him, he was like a kid. He had a huge smile on his face and he growled, "Hey! You guys body surf?" We said yes, and he jumped up and joined us as we went into the water. We usually body surfed the inside break and positioned ourselves to catch some waves. I took off on a nice shoulder and was getting a pretty good ride when I felt this big WHACK. I was stunned as I was knocked back into the wave. Coach Mahlstede had seen me take off and had positioned himself for a good "HIT" as I went by. He gave me a great forearm rip, and when I stood up in chest deep water, I saw him laughing his head off. "Great hit, huh, LaVigne. I really creamed ya!" That was the start of it. He soon got good licks in on all of us, so we decided to reciprocate.

He took off on a wave and my friend Rex really let him have it. Smash! He delivered a great forearm rip of his own! To our surprise, Coach Mahlstede got up and had an even bigger smile on his face. "Isn't this great!" And so began our little tradition of beating the hell out of each other at the beach! We would pride ourselves on getting a good hit or being quick or deceptive enough to avoid one of his. We would all get out of the water with scratches and scrapes, laughing while we recounted this wave or that forearm rip. It became very apparent that we had a very unique and special head coach.

During the time that I was playing football for Coach Mahlstede, my brother was at his worst. He was constantly getting into trouble.

He was arrested many times and his disrespect for my parents seemed to grow the more they tried to help him. There were times that he still attacked me, but he learned that I was older and stronger. He got a few ass beatings of his own.

I tried really hard to avoid conflict in our home. I just kept everything inside until one night during the middle of my junior football season. I came home from practice in mid-October to hear screaming and cursing from inside the house. My parents were trying to save my brother, but their strategy of patience and acceptance had finally reached its limit. As I walked through the hallway to my room, I heard my brother screaming and cursing at my mom and my dad. "Fuck you both. You bitch! You fucking whore! Shut the fuck up!" He then turned on my dad, "What the hell are going to do? I'll kick your fucking ass!" That was it! I had enough. I charged my brother in the hallway and drove him through the bathroom and into the bathtub. I was absolutely out of my mind. NOBODY talks to my parents like that…NOBODY! I had him in the bathtub, punching his face and his arms as he held them up to block my fists. I screamed at him as I was hitting him.

"NOBODY talks to Mom and Dad like that, you fucking asshole!" It was ugly. What was even uglier was my parents' reaction. They were yelling and screaming at ME! At ME!!! How could I do this to my brother? What was wrong with me? They pulled me back and went to HIS aid. They were yelling at me, telling me that I was the problem. I couldn't believe it. I don't know if I've ever felt that abandoned or betrayed.

I walked out of the house, crying like a baby. I was hurt, not physically, but deep in my heart. I was simply defending my parents in their own home, doing what I thought I was supposed to do. I was confused, hurt, and empty. I walked down my street and ended up at the only place that made me feel good, the football field at my high school. I sat for the longest time next to the shot put ring behind one of the goal posts and fell asleep. I woke up the next morning to the sound of cars passing by the street that bordered our practice field. There wasn't enough time to go home and change, so I went to the locker room, took a shower, put on the same clothes as the day before, and then went to class.

I was a TA, teacher's assistant, for Coach Mahlstede in the morning. He must have noticed something was wrong because he took me aside and talked to me. I don't remember what he said or what I said or if I even told him what had happened the night before. All I remember is that after he talked to me, I felt better. He made me feel that everything was going to be all right. It was at that moment that I knew that I wanted to be a teacher and a football coach just like him: strong yet compassionate, demanding yet encouraging. He opened up my eyes to a real and tangible goal, to be a teacher and a coach.

Looking back, I'm really surprised that my mom and dad didn't call the police or SOMEONE when I didn't come home the night before. Maybe they were too upset. Maybe they didn't even realize that I was gone. Maybe they didn't care. Whatever it was, I made it through the day and practice before going back home.

Coach Jack Mahlstede and his wife Billie

As time went by, Coach Mahlstede learned about me as well as my family. He saw the problems that I was having and went out of his way to make me feel special and valued. He included me as a part of his own family, taking me on camping trips, excursions to

Olvera Street, and football games. During my senior year, he and his wife Billie actually took my girlfriend and me on a "double date" to a beautiful restaurant several miles away for dinner after the prom. I still remember seeing swans for the first time in my life through large windows as we sat together at this very fancy restaurant. He also knew that my family did not have much money, so he found ways to help me by paying me to babysit his sons and do little odd jobs at his house. His rough exterior did not reflect his huge heart and deep compassion. He was a great coach but an even better human being.

I witnessed Coach Mahlstede's influence on other students and athletes as well. It was common to see him in private conversations with my classmates and teammates. I watched him listen intently to others who also had heavy burdens to bear. These sessions would always end with him hugging these troubled teenagers and then giving positive final words as they walked away. It was this genuine concern for "his boys" that made him an incredible teacher and coach, inspiring all of us to believe in ourselves and persevere. He led Santa Fe to more championships than any coach in the history of the school. Yes. His knowledge of football as well as his constant expectations for us to work hard and do our best made us winners on the field, but it was his sincere love for us and belief in us that made us champions in life.

Coach Mahlstede's powerful and positive impact on literally thousands of young men is best illustrated by an event that takes place every spring. At the beginning of trout season, over a hundred former players and coaches drive five hours to be with him, fishing on the streams of Bishop, California. The main reason every former player and coach goes on this trip is not to fish, but to spend time with his old coach and hero. It is a gesture of love and respect for a man that I have never seen anywhere else.

Jack Mahlstede taught me many things. He drilled into my head that desire and intensity can lead to great achievements. I learned that I had to sacrifice to be successful, doing things I didn't want to do, but had to do if I wanted to realize my dreams. He is the best example of how love and intensity can work as partners to achieve greatness. He taught me how to be a winner: to believe in myself and live life with passion, purpose, and grit.

10

SACRIFICE

*"There is no greater love than this:
that a person would lay down his life
for the sake of his friends."*

John 15:13

#55 STEVE SANCHEZ

My last coaching job was at La Serna High School. When I first arrived at the school, I met a young man named Stephen Sanchez. He was a junior, a solid football player and an incredible human being. He was a center, an offensive lineman, who had that unselfish, playful, and down-to-earth attitude that seems to come more often in offensive linemen than in any other position. He was also a student in my eleventh-grade English class. I still remember where he sat, right in the front row. I can still see him there in my mind, smiling and laughing with natural ease. He was a leader and a peacemaker. He seemed to always go out of his way to diffuse arguments and to make sure that everyone got along. He was also unselfish in a way uncommon to sixteen-year-olds. He always seemed to be much more concerned about the welfare of those around him than what he wanted. Little did I know that his leadership and unselfishness would become so important to not only his team but to every team that would follow him.

Steve Sanchez was an only child. His mother, Claudine, and his aunt, Marie, were fixtures on our sideline during games, taking pictures of Steve and all the other boys. They would share these pictures with smiles that only come from people who get great joy in giving to others. I've heard it said that there are two kinds of people in this world: givers and takers. Steve, his mother, and his aunt were most definitely givers.

Steve completely bought into our team mantra, "I've got your back." When I came to La Serna, there was great disunity and very little player loyalty and devotion to others on the team. I believed that we needed to cultivate that sense of loyalty as well as a tough-ness and determination to never back away from a challenge. It worked. Our players became more unselfish and dedicated to the team, leading to success on the field. At the time, I didn't realize that this concept of sacrifice and devotion would extend far beyond the scope of a football team.

At three o'clock in the morning a little over a year after Steve graduated, I received a phone call from one of his teammates. That teammate was in jail, as were several others who were Steve's team-mates and friends. Each of the boys was taken into custody by the Sheriff's Department and given one phone call. Much to the dis-may of this boy's mother, he chose to make that single phone call to me, his coach. "Steve's dead! Coach, he's dead!" The voice on the other end of that call came from a big, tough lineman. His voice cracked and he was crying. His friend, his teammate was dead. The voice's owner and his other friends were at a jail after having been taken in for questioning in an attempt to unravel what had hap-pened the night before.

There had been a party, one of those teenage bashes that is advertised with flyers and on social media attended by tons of kids who don't even know the person throwing the party. I hated those parties...still do. My players knew that, but a coach's influence is no match for friends' assurances that "It's no big deal. Nothing will happen," but things do happen at those parties and too many times, the end result is bad. This time, the results were deadly.

It was late in the night when Steve and a couple of his friends were leaving the party to go home. They were at his truck, almost ready to get in, when they heard all Hell break loose at the party. They turned to see a fight, a melee, which looked like one of those barroom brawls you see on television westerns. They saw their friends, their former teammates, surrounded by a crowd of other boys, throwing punches and fighting off an attack by a bunch of strangers. Steve and his friends went back. They started throwing their own punches. Steve took a position directly behind his friend and former quarterback, going back-to-back to get his friends out of trouble. The last thing that anybody ever heard him say was to his quarterback. "I've got your back." A few minutes later, Steve Sanchez was lying on the street dead. He had been stabbed in the back by someone he didn't even know.

In the frenzy and confusion, this piece of scum snuck up behind him and shoved a knife into his back; and now, the young man with the quick and easy smile, the one who always cared more about others than himself, the only child of a single mother, lay dead on the street.

Claudine, Steve's mother, who was ironically a Sheriff's deputy, learned about her son's death from fellow deputies who must have gone through Hell to tell this wonderful woman that the joy of her life, her beautiful son, would not be coming home anymore. I can only imagine how terrible that moment was for her, how her face must have contorted in disbelief and horror.

Days later, I learned something that had an effect on me that I can't even express, something that told me that what we do in coaching and playing a silly little sport is more important than I had ever imagined. Claudine had given a message to Steve's friends and relatives, "In lieu of flowers, please make a donation to the La Serna Touchdown Club." The Touchdown Club is our school's football booster club! How could a mother who had just lost her only child even think to make such a request? I called Claudine to express my deep sympathy and sadness and to ask why she had done such a thing. She told me that La Serna football, next to his deep faith in God and his love for his mother, was the most important thing in his life. She had a request of me.

"Please don't let them forget my son."

On the day of the funeral, our entire team waited in the team room before we left together. As Steve had done on game days when he played for our team, our players wore their crimson game day shirts. They sat in silence as the time to leave neared. Just before we were about to get into our cars and make our way to the church, there was a knock on the door. I answered the door to find some of Steve's former teammates standing there in shirts that commemorated their fallen friend. With tears in his eyes, Thomas asked if they could come in. I didn't say a word as I shook my head yes. Thomas, Dylan, Marcos, and other former players entered the room silently, slowly, and with great reverence. They moved about the room looking up at the pictures and posters that hung on the walls. They reached out with unsteady hands and touched team artifacts and trophies that stood on the bookshelves. They didn't say a word and neither did anyone else. They all began to weep and then looked at me with wrinkled faces and teary eyes. I tried to control my own tears and sadness while I hugged them. Then they left. Within a minute, the players stood and silently filed out of the room as well.

The funeral service was at a local church that Steve, his mother, and his aunt attended. I fought hard against what seemed to be an uncontrollable grief. I couldn't talk and because of the tears that I couldn't stop, I was barely able to see. As we drove to the church, I prayed that I would not be asked to speak because I knew that I would not be able to control my emotions. I would not be able to get through a single sentence without breaking down.

We arrived at the church and there were so many people there! It was a big church, but there were not enough seats for everyone to sit. People stood in the aisles and overflowed through the back doors. I had never seen so many people at a funeral before. Claudine had arranged to have a section in the front of the church reserved for our team, and we were led to our seats. During this entire time, I kept praying, "Please, Lord. Please don't have them ask me to speak. Please!" I loved this kid so much and my chest was tight and heart hurt more than I could have ever imagined! I was a mess.

When the service began, the pastor stood in front of this huge crowd, led us in prayer, and then told everyone that Steve's mother wanted some special people to talk about her son. "Coach LaVigne, would you please come up and say a few words?"

Oh my God! I didn't know how I was going to do that, and then I prayed, "Dear Lord, please give me the peace I need to honor this boy and his family. Please God!" I know that, to many, this may sound weird or fabricated, but as God as my witness, I immediately felt a complete calm fall over me. I stood up and spoke about a young man I respected and loved for several minutes. As I finished, that calm left me as I walked back to my seat with my team. He gave me what I needed to do a job that needed to be done. That was and still is the most spiritual moment of my life.

Hundreds upon hundreds of dollars began pouring in from people who had never even attended a La Serna football game. These donations came out of respect for a deeply sad friend and grieving mother. I made a decision on what to do for that mother and her son. I sketched out an idea for a flag that would symbolize what our football program is all about: unity, respect, hard work, and dedication. I brought the sketch to a local store that specialized in flags. They stocked all types of flags and actually created custom flags as well. I explained the situation and showed my sketch to the owner. Weeks later, I picked up our flag. It was beautiful, a full-sized flag with a coat of arms in the middle broken into quadrants with the four symbols of our team and program. Our motto, "Courage. Character. Commitment." was prominently printed across it and at the bottom, it read, "In honor and memory of Steve Sanchez #55". From that point on, the flag was carried onto the field by our captain as the team took the field at the beginning of the game and after halftime at every game I coached. Even years after I stopped coaching, that tradition and show-of-respect continues.

During the game, the flag is displayed next to our bench on the sideline, and at the beginning of every season, our players were told about the flag's history and what it meant to all of us. After every game we won, it was carried to the top of the steps at our school where we announced that week's player of the game. In front of hundreds of parents, players, coaches, and supporters, that player would climb the stairs, attach the embroidered name of the school we beat to the Velcro strip along the side of the flag, and it was waved in victory amidst the clapping and cheering of our La Serna family. It became a big part of our tradition. I am grateful that future coaches who replaced me have kept that tradition alive.

We also had a huge perpetual trophy made for our new award, the "Steve Sanchez Memorial Award" given to the varsity player who sacrificed the most for his teammates. It is the last trophy given at the varsity awards banquet after the Most Valuable Player award. When we present it each year, Claudine, Steve's mother, attends the banquet as we retell his story and explain the significance of this award, telling parents, players, and friends that this was the most prestigious honor given in our program.

The large trophy remains in the team room, and other versions were made. A plaque is given to each year's recipient and a second trophy was given to Steve's mother. It became a practice for Claudine to share her trophy with Steve's friends who would each keep it for a month before turning it over to another one of his friends and teammates for another month. Claudine took the

In Memory of
Steve Sanchez

SANCHEZ
55

*Steve's parents, Coach LaVigne, and family members
celebrate his life when his jersey was retired.*

money from Steve's life insurance, put it into a bank account, and gave a check to the player who received the award each year to go toward his college education. What an incredible thing to do…and what an incredible person she is!

I gave this award to every Steve Sanchez Memorial Trophy recipient for many years following his death. In the years that have followed my retirement from coaching, I continue to be asked to describe this award's significance before it is presented at each varsity football banquet. When I do, I emphasize that we are not glorifying fighting at parties. I also tell the athletes attending the banquet that they should never attend parties that are advertised and promoted by people they don't know. What I do tell them is that one of their own gave his life to defend a teammate, and that this type of loyalty and sacrifice is the greatest gift that anyone can give to another.

Although La Serna has had outstanding football players who went on to greatness in college and the NFL, there are only two football jerseys that have been retired at our school. One of those jerseys is that of Steve Sanchez #55. That pretty much says it all.

11

DEVOTION

"Devotion is diligence without assurance."

~ Elizabeth Gilbert

DIEGO

The boys who have won the Steve Sanchez Memorial Award are all special. Some were great players and some were good. All of them had tremendous character. It has been given to players who were the Most Valuable Players of our team and league; and it has been given to others, some all-league and some not. One boy is perhaps the best example of what this award is all about.

Diego played football for four years at La Serna. He was a good player but not a great one. He started some games, but not too many. He was just a good, tough kid who always gave his best. Diego was in my first period English class during his junior year. Right after the holidays, he started coming to school late once or twice a week. I warned him to stop being tardy, and he got better, but the problem persisted. After one of his tardies, I brought him outside my classroom and asked him why he was having so much trouble getting to school on time. He really didn't want to tell me. He didn't want to give excuses. He said that he'd get better and make sure to get to school on time.

He got better at getting to school on time but was still occasionally late to class. Once more, I brought him outside the classroom and asked him what the heck was going on. It was then that he told me.

I learned that his stepfather had abandoned his family, leaving him, his mother, and his younger brother and sister with bills that could no longer be paid. Their situation was desperate. To solve the problem, his mother had decided to move the family in with relatives about forty miles away. If he went with his mother and siblings, he would have a stable home and an easy commute to his new school, but he didn't want to go. He wanted to stay at La Serna and play his senior football season at his own school. His mother was not happy with his decision, but he persisted. His mother said that his only other option was to move in with his uncle who lived closer, but still about twenty miles from La Serna. His uncle had a small apartment in a bad neighborhood and very little money. If Diego wanted to continue to go to La Serna, he would have to arrange his own transportation. He did.

Diego decided to stay with his uncle. In order to get to La Serna on time, he had to get up at 3:30 AM every morning to warm up a can of soup to eat for breakfast, pack whatever there was for lunch, and walk (sometimes run) to the bus stop for his first bus to school. It took three buses to get to La Serna by 8:00 AM. If the buses were late, so was he. If it rained, he got wet, and when the day was done, he retraced his bus routes back home to that small apartment in a very tough area of town. Most nights, he got home at 8:00 or 9:00 PM. It was almost a ridiculous commitment, but one he wanted to make.

During the rest of his junior year and throughout his senior year, Diego never missed a practice or workout He also never complained, and he was always the hardest working player on the team. Sometimes, he was able to spend the night at a friend's house or, after going to his church near the school, he was allowed to sleep over at his minister's house. When that wasn't possible, he still did not miss his weekly youth ministry sessions at church, but simply took a later, much later, bus ride home. Through it all, Diego always had a smile on his face and never, absolutely never complained or lamented about his difficult situation. He wanted to be at La Serna and he wanted to play for its football team. To say that he was dedicated is an incredible understatement.

I took Diego home whenever I could, and each time, I was amazed at not only the distance, but with the mean, gang-infested streets he had to traverse to make his twice-daily commutes. His plight broke my heart, and his positive attitude inspired me every day. One night, I took Diego home after a game. When we made the turn down the small, dark street to his apartment, we saw lights, police cars, ambulances, and crime scene tape surrounding the parking lot of his run-down apartment complex.

There had been a triple murder just outside the window where Diego slept. I offered to take him home, but he wouldn't hear of it. He smiled and told me to let him off. He could talk his way into his apartment. I couldn't believe it, but he insisted, and sure enough, I watched as he made his way around the bright yellow tape and into his apartment. He was at practice…on time…the next day.

Diego told me about times he walked to or from his apartment when it was dark, and a car would slow down and pull up next to him. He learned not to respond to the voices coming out of the cars. He learned to never look up and establish eye contact. There were only a couple times that his tactics didn't work. He got jumped and beaten up once; and another time, there was a brief scuffle and his backpack was stolen. When he told me this, I was shocked. I told him that he was lucky he didn't get shot, but be said it was "no big deal." The gangsters in the area had gotten to know him and he was not a real threat, so he was "mostly safe".

I remember thinking that so many other boys missed school or practice for such trivial reasons, and that I could not imagine ANYONE going through what he did to just be a part of a school and football team. To this day, I cannot think of anyone who deserved the Steve Sanchez Memorial Award more than Diego.

When I gave him his award at our awards banquet after his senior season and described his sacrifice and dedication, 350 people stood up and gave Diego a standing ovation. Everyone stood up but one person, his mother, who was sitting at his table. She remained seated and looked as though she was angry, bitter, and embarrassed. I don't know why she acted that way; I can only guess. All I can say is that it was happy and sad at the same time. It was happy because all Diego's teammates, their parents, and his coaches recognized his character and determination. It was sad because the one person Diego wanted to please most just sat there...and didn't even clap. Once again, Diego broke my heart and inspired me at the same time.

12

COMMITMENT

*"We have to recognize that there cannot be
relationships unless there is commitment,
unless there is loyalty, unless there is love, patience, persistence."*

~ Cornel West

OASIS

In the process of trying to influence my decision to accept this new assignment to build a program for at-risk students, our principal Martin Plourde and had me travel to Adlai Stevenson High School in Illinois with several other teachers, counselors, and administrators from our district. Stevenson High School had (and continues to have) tremendous success in the academic development of its students. They also have a program called the Mentor Program that deals specifically with at-risk students and was led by an extremely dedicated and unselfish teacher whose name is Sandi Millman.

On our trip, we had the opportunity to spend just a little time with Sandi Millman to discuss the basics of her program. She was generous in giving us materials she uses in working with her struggling students, and this information eventually became crucial in the development of our own program.

On the plane ride back home from Stevenson High School, I asked my principal what he wanted our program to look like. His answer was perfect. It was liberating and empowering and motivated me more than I could have imagined. He said, "Make it whatever you want it to be." Wow! That response lit my fuse, and we took off.

We created a program that has many of the characteristics of what we saw at Adlai Stevenson High School, but it is different in many ways. Since I am an old, broken-down football coach, I have some very specific things that I feel are important to incorporate into OASIS, which stands for Organized Academic Support In School. The best teachers I have ever had in my life have been coaches. What they taught me and what they gave me were things that made a huge difference in my life.

Although I had always been a good student, I was really an at-risk kid myself many years ago. Many of my childhood friends drank, took drugs, stole things, fought, and were headed down a path that I was following, too. What pulled me off that path was the guidance of some great men. What they taught me were things that I learned to apply to not only the football field, but to the classroom and to my life. Their impact was unmistakable, and I want to make the same type of impact on the students in our OASIS program.

Like so many other teachers and coaches, I have always struggled with the "why".

- Why does this student or athlete not care?

- Why does he continue to cut school, not do his homework, take drugs, drink, verbally abuse others, and give such little effort in something as important as school or sports?

- Why is he so angry, inconsistent, rude, apathetic, confrontational, or unmotivated?

- Why can I get through to one student but not to another student?

- What do I have to do to make these young people understand?

The answers to these questions are at the heart of any educational program, especially one that addresses the needs of at-risk students. Now, it is my job to answer these questions if the program I was asked to direct is to be successful.

I'm not foolish enough to believe that I have the final solution, the magic formula that will transform our most disinterested, failing students into motivated learners and accomplished scholars. I do believe, however, that I have a plan, a plan that incorporates the most essential components of student success. These critical components are not things that are typically seen as academic goals. At first sight, they probably appear to be vague, general principles that are nice, but not specific to academic performance. That could not be further from the truth. These essential components are the pillars on which any successful curriculum should be built. Teaching these principles and incorporating them into every lesson taught in a classroom lays the foundation of a lifetime of academic, personal, and professional success.

"Give a man a fish, and he will eat for a day.
Teach a man to fish, and he will eat for a lifetime."

This quote initially appeared in the Christian Science Monitor in 1965, and it is at the core of what education should be. Teaching vocabulary, mathematical equations, and important historical events have obvious value; but these lessons are finite in nature and do not sustain continued learning or promote meaningful application of that learning. There is something more to education than that! Effective teachers lead their students to ask "why" and "how". Teaching is preparation for life. What do we want our students to be and think and do when they are adults? We want them to be honest,

responsible, caring, independent thinkers. We want them to be fulfilled and productive members of society. We need to instill in them
a passion for learning that stays with them for a lifetime.

We built our OASIS program with this in mind, employing
student volunteer academic mentors to guide struggling students
through the process. I established daily and weekly protocols that
provide structure and balance to their learning. We maintain regular
communication between students, teachers, counselors, and parents
that facilitate an ongoing support system that nurtures their development. Most importantly, we focus on core values that we incorporate into their instruction, principles that will hopefully allow them
to "…eat for a lifetime."

I define and illustrate these values to my students. They are the
foundation of learning, growth, and success. Do all students buy
what I'm selling? No. It is difficult to break fifteen years of bad habits
in one school year; yet, we have had great success with the majority
of our students, using these principles as our foundation.

During our first year, thirty-two tenth graders were placed in
OASIS. When these students progressed to their eleventh grade year,
we added forty more sophomores and maintained support for our
remaining juniors. (Yes, some of them didn't make it to the eleventh
grade, but most did.) In the third year of OASIS, we added more
sophomores while providing support for our juniors and seniors.
During this period of time, the grade point average of our students
rose from 0.93 to 2.46. Attendance for these students improved
to over 90 percent, and citizenship grades improved dramatically.
Our methodology is constantly being refined, but the foundation of
what we do with these students remains consistent. This foundation
involves much of what my coaches taught me as well as my teammates many years ago.

Not all of my coaches were necessarily great teachers, but most
of them were. I learned what not to do from the ones who discour-
aged my teammates and me. I did, however, have some amazing
coaches whose leadership, guidance, and example inspired and

motivated me. The memory of them and what I learned from them is fundamental to what I try to instill in my students.

In my early years as a coach, I made a lot of mistakes in how I treated and taught my players. The feeling that I had to be tough, stubborn, and needlessly demanding many times overshadowed my basic instinct to simply teach. As the years progressed, I abandoned many of the practices that I employed as a young coach. Don't get me wrong. I never became the perfect example of what a coach should be, but I did improve every year in nurturing my players as human beings and students first and football players second. I learned that I was at my best when I was positive, patient, encouraging, balanced, and under control. As the years rolled by, the things my coaches taught me became more and more meaningful and relevant. These principles helped me become a better coach, teacher, and role model.

Working with at-risk students all day every day is a true blessing but it is also exhausting. Each student has his own unique set of challenging circumstances to overcome. Anger, apathy, and resistance wear me down every day. On many days, this job sucks the brains out of my head and tests me in ways I have never been tested before. It is beyond teaching. It is establishing a family with common goals and values, many of which have never been taught in these kids' homes. There is not a week that goes by that I don't sit, talk, and cry privately with at least a couple students who tell me about horrific things they have to endure all the time. I constantly have to recalibrate my brain and heart so that I have something to give the next kid. I drive home and get pep talks and reassuring words from my incredible wife Gisele all the time. I do my best, knowing that my best is often not good enough.

As educators, we teach kids. We teach students who are people, young people who struggle with balancing work and play, young people who have varying degrees of self-doubt. We teach kids who desperately yearn for sincerity, compassion, guidance, structure, and encouragement. We teach young people who will remember things that are said and done in our classrooms and on the athletic fields much longer and more strongly than we will. We teach kids who will be adults someday. What will they remember? What kind of people will they become? Will they feel motivated and empowered in our classroom or will they simply try to survive? It's important that they learn subject-verb agreement, how many planets there are in our solar system, and the primary causes of World War II; but we have a bigger responsibility, a greater mission. It's our job to teach their minds, but it is infinitely more important that we touch their hearts and coach their souls.

13

WISDOM AND POWER

"Knowing others is intelligence;
knowing yourself is true wisdom.
Mastering others is strength;
mastering yourself is true power."

~ La Tzu

"Power is of two kinds. One is obtained by the fear of
punishment and the other by acts of love. Power based on love
is a thousand times more effective and permanent than the
one derived from fear of punishment."

~ Mahatma Gandhi

THE CIRCLE

As a teacher, there is something I have done in my classroom for many years that really sets the tone for all of the time we spend together. It's my best lesson as a teacher. I do this activity on a day during the first week of school, and it has made all the difference in the world. Although I teach the most at-risk students in our school, I have written only a few referrals for behavior in the past fifteen years. The reason for this is definitely not because my students are afraid of me. On the contrary, it is pretty common for my students to poke fun at me and laugh with me about something silly that I say or do. I truly believe that the biggest reason for me having few behavioral problems in my classroom is because of the love and respect that I have for them and the love and respect that they return to me. It all starts with the activity that I will describe. It's called "The Circle".

I have my students sit in a big circle, facing the center of the classroom. I stand in the middle and ask them to imagine that I am a blind person who has never been in the classroom before. I hear everyone say that it is a nice room, but because I am blind, I have to depend upon them to tell me what makes it so nice. I ask four different students who are each seated at different points in the circle, "What is in the room?" I tell the students that they must each answer the question honestly but can only tell me what they see … AND they cannot turn their head. I obviously get four different answers. One student will say, "There's a flag, a door, and a couch." Another will say, "There are five computers, a leadership banner, and a football helmet." I receive four distinctly different answers. After hearing their responses, I say, "Someone is lying to me! I asked everyone sitting in the same room the same question and received four totally different answers. Therefore, someone MUST be lying! Is that correct?"

That question is always met with many confused faces and a few hands raised in the air. I call on a waving hand, and that student says loudly, "No! We're not lying."

"Well then," I ask, "how can I get four different answers to that same question if we are all sitting in the same room?" Another raised hand leads to an answer more insightful than they know, "It's because we each have a different perspective." Aha!

We talk about that revelation and I go to each of the four students and ask the same two questions, "Were you telling me the TRUTH?"

and "Is your truth better than his or her truth?" I ask this second question while pointing to a student who answered differently.

The answer to the first question is always "Yes" and the answer to the second question is always "No." We then discuss the fact that life is exactly like that circle. We all sit in our "seat" in life and see things in a completely unique way.

Discussion leads us to the realization that our seat is determined by our genetic makeup and all the experiences (good and bad) that we have had in our lives. We each see things uniquely. No one can ever sit in our "seat" and see things exactly as we do. Therefore, truth is relative and no person has exclusive rights to it. We have to respect the fact that others may be telling the truth, but that truth is completely different than our own. Although we can never see things exactly as someone else does, we can come very, very close if we do something, something that is one of the most powerful things that we can do as human beings, **listen**.

I tell my students that **wisdom** is measured and determined by how well we see things from the perspectives of others. As an English teacher, I used to tell my students to always write from their own "seats", sharing their unique perspectives. As a human being, I remind them (and myself) quite often that no one OWNS the truth; but if we do this powerful thing, listen, we can learn more and more of the truth, becoming truly wise. The natural by-product of this exercise is the development of respect, trust, and some pretty darn good listening skills. It has made my classroom a very cool place for a long time. We also use this activity as a springboard to a very important lesson about "power".

I ask my students to close their eyes and think of the person that they love and respect more than anyone in the world. They don't share the identity of that person with anyone. I just ask them to think about him or her. I tell my students that I bet this person is not necessarily someone who is rich or popular or beautiful. I tell them that I bet this person is someone who loves them, respects them, places their needs above their own, and tries to see things from their perspective.

I ask my students if I am correct, and so far, I've always been right. Then, I ask them to imagine that they are standing in the front room of their home, looking out onto the front yard or court-yard of their apartment where this person is standing. As they are looking out at that person, 10 to 12 tough-looking guys approach with chains, clubs, and knives. Then, as they watch, these guys begin beating this person who they love unmercifully. I then ask, "What do you do?"

The answer is always the same. They say that they would run through the door and defend this person, fighting off the attackers. Every time, some students say they wouldn't even wait for the door. They would jump through the window to protect this loved, respected person. Then I say, "Wait a minute! You might be hurt! You might be killed!"

Their response is consistent, "It doesn't matter." I tell them that this person who is being defended has tremendous "power". They would risk being hurt or killed in an instant to defend this loved one. That is TRUE POWER. For someone to be so important that a person would be willing, without hesitation, to risk his or her life to defend them is to be truly powerful. I ask my students where that power comes from. It didn't come from wealth, popularity, good looks, or cool clothes. This power, the power to make some-one willing to die in their defense, comes from that person's love, compassion, humility, and devotion. I tell them that, if they want to be truly powerful, they have to be caring, unselfish, humble, and open-minded. Good lesson!

On a side note, I coached football for years, and I shared this activity with many teams. At the end of the activity, I would tell them to earn this power from each other with patience, kindness, and unselfishness. Then, I'd tell them that when they see each other, as teammates, in the same way that they envisioned that loved one being attacked … when they cared THAT much about each other, they could never get beat.

14

COURAGE

*"It takes a great deal of bravery to stand up
to our enemies, but just as much
to stand up to our friends."*

~J.K. Rowling

SANTIAGO

I heard a lot about Santiago before I even met him. He had been kicked out of his first high school during his freshman year for having a knife on campus, transferring to La Serna for a new start. That new start wasn't going so well when he was assigned to me at the beginning of his sophomore year. He had failed virtually all of his classes during his freshman year. I was warned by teachers who knew him that, "He doesn't care." They said, "He won't do anything in class. He's sneaky. Watch yourself!"

I was taking on this new responsibility and naturally assumed that if I was to be working with at-risk kids, Santiago had to be in that group. Some well-meaning teachers who felt that their experience with Santiago would help me avoid some of the difficult situations they had encountered with him cautioned me about him. The fact is, though, I really didn't pay too much attention because I wanted to make up my own mind.

On the first day of class that year, Santiago entered my class-room with his two best friends, Hugo and Adrian. They all had that first-day look on their faces, smiling, joking, and acting cool, but unable to disguise just a bit of anxious apprehension. Hugo was tall and athletic looking with a sort of sinister smile but an engaging personality. He liked to look the part of the gangster with baggy pants, white tee shirt, and brand new baseball cap sitting at various angles on his head depending upon the day. Adrian was also tall but much thinner than his two friends and wore clothes not quite as edgy as his two buddies. He seemed to have a perpetual "happy-goofy" expression that made it difficult to take him seriously at times.

Santiago was altogether different in appearance. He was fairly tall and stocky with a typical crew cut that distinguishes but is not exclusive to gangsters. His round face and squinting eyes were a bit menacing, exposing some long-simmering bitterness and distrust inside him. His eyes scanned the room without his head turning, and there was no smile on his face like his two friends. As they sat down, he glanced at others periodically as though to make sure no one was sneaking up on him. He looked like an interesting young man.

"How's it goin', young man?" I asked as I passed out the year's first round of papers.

"Awright. Hey, what is this shit, anyway?" He asked without looking me square in the eyes. He wasn't comfortable in a classroom setting and his question challenged me as I slid past him to continue my obligatory job of distributing the class rules and syllabus.

I stopped to answer, "Well, you haven't been doing too well in school, and now it's my job to get you on track."

"Sheeeit!" he replied without even looking up. That was my first interaction with Santiago. For the next several weeks, he sat quietly and tentatively in my classroom as I tried to reassure him and his classmates that I was not the enemy but their ally and friend. I wanted Santiago and my other students to know that we were going to work together, to give them reasons to try hard in school, and that I would provide all the support possible to help them. None of that impressed him as he sat day after day, without engaging anyone in conversation other than his two buddies and a few other students he already knew.

Weeks turned into months, and Santiago gradually began to trust me and showed at least incidental interest in what we were doing in class. That didn't change much until a week in early November. I had my students keep a journal in class to express their feelings about their situations as well as other topics I felt were important for them to consider. The last journal entry of the week in early November was, "What would you attempt if you knew that you wouldn't fail?" As was my practice, I took the journals home for the weekend to read them before the next week of class. I was encouraged to read the unusually long response in Santiago's journal. He said that, if he KNEW that he wouldn't fail, he would box. He wrote about how he loved boxing just like his father and would love to train as a boxer and slug it out with others, showing that he was tough and strong. I was impressed but unsure of how I would use this information to motivate him. I didn't have to wait long for an answer.

On the following Monday morning, I saw that the red light on my phone was blinking, indicating that I had at least one phone message. I picked up the receiver and pushed the buttons to hear what I considered to be a surprising message that bordered on a miracle. The message was from Danny Zamora, a young man I had coached at Santa Fe fifteen years earlier. Danny was a small but extremely tough kid, weighing about 145 pounds when I met him at Santa Fe. Before I knew him, he had been a highly successful boxer in a youth program, winning major tournaments and titles until a severe shoulder injury prematurely ended his once promising boxing career. In a move that showed my true ignorance, I encouraged him to play football for us. Nice move, Coach LaVigne! You take a guy with shoulder problems and convince him to play football! That wasn't the smartest thing I've ever done, but it was definitely one of the best.

Danny started as our quick side defensive end and excelled beyond anyone's expectations. His quickness, toughness, and tenacity made him an all-star and one of our best defensive players. He and I became very close, and I was honored just to know him. After graduating from high school, Danny returned to boxing as a trainer, working himself up from apprentice positions to the director of The Santa Fe Springs Youth Boxing Program. His talent and dedication led him to prominence, training two world champion fighters. In Danny's phone message, he said that he had read an article in our local newspaper, describing our at-risk program run by his old coach. He called to tell me that he was excited to read this and asked if he could come to La Serna and talk to my kids.

I called him back, telling him how great it was to hear from him after all these years and to extend an invitation for him to come speak to my students. Within a week, he was standing in my classroom with his big smile and a much-appreciated hug for his old coach.

Before he spoke to the students, I gave him a quick review of our program and the kids it was to serve. I also mentioned the uncanny coincidence of Santiago's journal entry. I introduced him, and he took control of the class. He told them of his personal adversity in losing his dream of becoming a professional boxer years earlier and how it devastated him. He shared some very nice things about our relationship and how my belief in him helped him recover from an extremely dark period in his life. Then, he made an offer and issued a challenge.

"Coach LaVigne will help you if you let him, and I will help you, too. If you do everything Coach says, I will train you for free in my gym. All you have to do is get there. I will take care of the paperwork and waive all the fees, but if I ever hear from Coach that you are slacking off in class and not doing what he says, I'll kick you out of my program."

As he spoke, I saw something in Santiago' eyes that I had never seen before. He was attentive and interested. His eyes became more and more excited as Danny spoke. Santiago and four of his classmates, including Hugo and Adrian, decided to take him up on his offer. They organized rides among them and began training with Danny at his gym. I was elated by their interest and relieved that they would receive much-needed extra brainwashing from someone as impressive and inspiring as Danny. This band of five kids continued their training at the gym, and although none of them ever became a top competitor in the ring, all five went through a huge transformation of spirit, becoming respectful and successful students. A few years later, they all graduated from La Serna. Danny's influence on them was obvious, and I told him so every chance I got.

Santiago underwent the biggest transformation. He no longer was that angry, distrustful tough guy, sitting passively in my classroom while glaring at anyone other than his few trusted friends. He became friendly and helpful, leading classmates in group activities and even volunteering to help pass out papers or empty overflowing trash cans in my classroom. What made his transformation even more amazing was the fact that he lost two of his closest friends to gang violence during that first year we spent together. One of his "homies" was shot in a drive-by and the other was killed in a confrontation between two rival gangs. I worried that these two deeply painful incidents would draw Santiago back to his previous identity as a gangster who felt obliged to avenge his friends' murders. I was shocked and inspired by Santiago's reaction. Instead of falling victim to the violence that had permeated his life before joining us, Santiago made the conscious decision to walk away from his gang and its destructive lifestyle.

Santiago decided that there was something better for him than his gang affiliation, and he "jumped out" of his gang. This process was especially brutal because it required him to be beaten and kicked into submission by others in his gang with whom he had not so long ago pledged total allegiance. This was even more courageous because of where Santiago lived, in an area that was bordered by three rival gangs. After going through this "jumping out" process, he no longer had to feel the unlawful obligations of his previous gang, but would no longer receive the protection of that gang from the threat of the other two groups. That took courage! It also took tremendous discipline and self-control.

Santiago started spending morning breaks and lunchtimes in my classroom, doing homework, playing his guitar, and sharing lunches with me. I asked him once why he was hanging out with the old guy every day and not spending his time on campus with his friends.

"No offense, Coach, but it's not just because of you. If I go out there, I'll probably get in a fight or do something stupid. I want to graduate."

That was the best possible response because it revealed remarkable growth and maturity in a kid who was, just months before, someone who could care less about goals and dreams. I wanted to reward him and my other at-risk students for their success, so I planned a "Reward Field Trip". I wanted to take Santiago and his classmates somewhere they had never been, so I asked them one day, "Okay, guys. I want to take you on a cool field trip to celebrate everything you've done. Where do you want to go?"

Santiago's response may not have reflected appropriate school language, but it was priceless. "I wanna go to the fuckin' zoo!"

"You wanna go where?" I asked.

"You heard me, Coach. I wanna go to the zoo. I never been to a zoo and I think it would be cool." That declaration ignited the rest of the class who supported his choice. "Yeah! I never been to the zoo either. I want to see some fucking monkeys!" was one vote of support, followed by, "That would be fucking great, man! Hey, they got camels in a zoo?" I was shocked to hear that almost none of them had ever been to a zoo.

After reminding them that there were better words to express their excitement, I told them that we would go to the zoo. We took a busload of students to the Los Angeles County Zoo, and they absolutely loved it. They were like little kids as they walked and sometimes ran to different exhibits, watching gorillas, giraffes, and other exotic animals that they had only read about in books. Well, maybe they hadn't read about them as much as they had looked at the pictures, but that didn't matter. They loved the zoo and the entire experience.

Santiago did graduate and went on to get a part-time job while attending classes at Rio Hondo, our local community college. About a year after he received his diploma, he, Hugo, and Adrian paid me a visit. It was just before noon on a shortened school day, so we decided to go out to lunch together. It was fun and inspiring. As I sat at a table with these three young men who were once labeled as incorrigible, I felt tremendous admiration and pride, thinking of all the steps they had taken to get to this point. All three had been labeled as probable dropouts, but now, here we sat! All three of them graduated from high school, had jobs, and were attending college. What a great lunch!

15

PERSEVERANCE

"Sometimes even to live is an act of courage."

~ Seneca

ISABEL

Sometimes, children are pulled in a hundred different directions by things that are not conducive to success in school. Parents of too many of our students struggle financially just to survive, working jobs that pull them both away from the home and require their eldest children to pick up that slack by having jobs themselves and staying home from school to care for younger siblings. That was Isabel's situation, and it was obvious that the demands of home and school were weighing her down.

Isabel was a sweet, timid soul who never said more than a few softly spoken words to me during the entire three years I had her as a student at La Serna. She was attentive and respectful when she was in class, but the problem was that she missed school almost as much as she attended. That obviously created a hopeless continuum of falling behind, catching up, and falling behind again and again.

Isabel was the oldest child in her family and was given the responsibility of caring for her younger brothers and sisters when both parents worked long hours at a thrift store that they precariously owned and operated. She was a compliant soldier in the war to survive that her family fought every day. She wanted to come to school, but knew that her first priority was her family. That's hard to argue, so convincing Isabel and her parents that the best way to serve her family was to do well in school, graduate, continue her education, and get a good job that would provide critical financial support in the home was a tough sell. What had to come first, however, was an awareness of her circumstances. Many of our students suffer through extreme difficulties that are not addressed, mainly because these difficulties are not known by teachers and counselors who are able to help. That was Isabel's situation until one late morning after class.

Most of the time, my classes are more like game shows or circus performances than the conventional atmospheres experienced during other periods. There is order and a plan, but it's just not the kind that most teachers employ. It's a complicated combination of immediate rewards given for academic achievements and a subtle system of indoctrination, establishing students' acceptance of critical values that serve as a foundation of success in all areas of their lives. One of the things I do is provide students with the opportunity to earn "Cookie Privileges" for achieving academic goals. Each week, I buy about 30 to 40 packages of cookies and 18 to 20 gallons of water for my sneaky plan to motivate my at-risk angels. Water jugs are placed in a big refrigerator we keep in the classroom, and a few cookie jars are constantly stocked with a variety of unhealthy but much-desired treats.

Students work with academic mentors, outstanding upperclassmen who volunteer a period every day to tutor, guide, and mentor their younger, struggling at-risk classmates. These students and mentors are divided into teams of 6 to 8 members with goals of improving attendance, behavior, and academic performance. Teams that reach their goals are given Cookie Privileges for the week, allowing members to have as many cookies and cups of cold water as they want during class. It may sound silly and juvenile, but it really does work. I have always found that kids, even teenagers, like both rewards and recognition and will work hard to earn them.

Toward the end of class one morning, Alyssa, Isabel's mentor, asked if she could talk to me privately. We stepped outside my classroom and with beautiful compassion, Alyssa asked me if I could make an exception for Isabel, allowing her to have Cookie Privileges during the week even though their team had not reached their goal. Alyssa told me that Isabel's family was really struggling, and that on some days, the cookies given to her during class were all she had to eat for the day. My jaw dropped and my eyes watered as I imagined this wonderful girl and her family being in such dire circumstances. "Of course!" I said, but I included that I wanted to talk to both of them after class. I told Alyssa to gather a bunch of cookies and surreptitiously give them to Isabel, reminding her to have Isabel stay for our little meeting.

When class ended, Isabel and Alyssa stayed behind and we spoke. "Listen, Isabel. Alyssa cares about you very much and is worried about you. Please don't be upset with her for telling me, but I know that things are rough for your family right now. First, I want you to promise me to never be hungry at school. I'm an old, mushy guy and one of the few things I do pretty well is to make sure that fantastic kids like you are taken care of. I want you to still work hard to achieve your weekly goals, but you may have cookies whenever you want them. All I ask is that you try hard in school, just like you're doing now. Secondly, I want you to go see your counselor at lunchtime today. I will call and speak with her before you get there. She's going to get you a card for the lunch program. That will give you a free breakfast and lunch every day. Use it! If I ever find out that you don't use it and are hungry, I'm gonna get really mad. Do you understand?"

She nodded her head yes and looked embarrassed. Noticing her expression, I reminded her of what a great kid she was and how much we loved her. I told her that my family struggled when I was young and I had free lunch, too. I told her that I had special teachers that took care of me the way I was going to take care of her, emphasizing that it was an honor and joy to do so. I reminded her again of what amazing people that she and her mentor were. When I finally got a smile and look of relief from Isabel, I sent them on their way.

It was beautiful to see them walk away together, sharing a friendship that would be life-changing for both of them. I immediately got on the phone and spoke to Isabel's counselor who not only placed Isabel in our free lunch program, but called her younger brother's and sister's school to make sure that they had free lunch as well. I was angry at myself for not noticing Isabel's situation on my own much earlier, but I was also grateful for the mentor, counselor, and free lunch program for helping this young girl. This was just another affirmation that as corny as it sounds, it really does "take a village".

I began calling Isabel's parents at their little store, telling them how much we respected and admired Isabel for her hard work and success and how much I respected them, her parents, for supporting Isabel's efforts by making sure that she attends school every day. This was a bit of manipulation and salesmanship on my part, knowing that it was her parents who almost always instigated Isabel's absences, requiring her to stay at home and tend to her baby sister. I wanted them to feel invested in Isabel's success at school. I always repeated my respect for their wishes and the importance of family, but continued to call whenever Isabel was absent, telling them how important her education was and how difficult it was for her to catch up after missing school. I also made sure to have extra sandwiches, granola bars, apples, and bananas in class to share with my shy, hungry little student who would eventually graduate from La Serna with a 3.0 grade point average.

16

CHARACTER

"The true test of a man's character
is what he does when no one is watching."

~ John Wooden

COACH SOUTH

Coming to Rio Hondo College to play football was not what I planned, but it turned out to be one of the best decisions I ever made. During my two years there, we were conference champions twice. We had four JC All Americans on both teams and more characters than I have ever met in my life, players and coaches. It was a totally different experience than high school. High school football had been great for me, but this was something totally different and totally unexpected.

One of our coaches at Rio Hondo stood out from all the rest. Our other three coaches were all good men in their own right and excellent coaches, too. Clint South was just someone totally unlike any other coach (or person) any of us had ever known. He was a tall man with a bald head; but, even though he was in his forties, you could see that he was a stud. He was wide-shouldered and had a small waist. We would always see him working out in the weight room, not to show off like some coaches do, but to just be with his players and to stay in shape. He had played football at UCLA for the famous coach, Red Sanders. He never volunteered that information, but gave it up when we asked him about his playing experience. His appearance was impressive, but that's not what made him so unique.

Clint South was our line coach, and he embodied all the things any player would ever want in a coach. There was nothing pretentious about him. You knew that what he told you was the truth, and that truth wouldn't change when he spoke to someone else. He was a quiet man; in all the time I've known him, I've never heard him yell, or lose control of himself. That is especially rare in a line coach. Line coaches are normally fiery, frenzied individuals who move, speak, and judge quickly. Clint South was none of those things. He was deliberate in what he said, and we quickly learned to listen to every word. He was a technician who had the uncommon knack to take something that was complicated and make it simple. He made our jobs as players easy. All we had to do was listen and execute the fundamental basics that he taught us. He never placated or patronized us, but he also never demeaned any player, either. He also never cussed, at least not in front of us. He believed in us, and his confidence made us better players and better people.

After playing for Coach South, he became the standard by which I judged myself and my coaches. I suppose the highest compliment that I can give anyone and the best way to explain my respect for him was the fact that, after playing for him, I decided that when I got married and had a son, I would name him Clint. I have two sons, and my first-born's name is Clint LaVigne.

It's hard to describe exactly how or why he was so good, and he certainly was an exceptional coach as well as human being. Several of his players became All-Americans, and I have never known anyone who has played for him who did not think that he was the best coach he had ever encountered. His linemen went on to earn scholarships to places like USC, UCLA, Nebraska, Washington State, and Colorado; and every lineman that he coached, to a man, would have given up that scholarship to continue playing for him if Rio Hondo became a four-year college. The things that made him so great had more to do with his character than his football knowledge or coaching ability. He was genuine, sincere, positive, and strong. We all loved him.

He used to lift weights and play handball with us, competing on the handball court with every bit of the intensity that we had. Other coaches also played handball with us and were equally competitive, but Coach South always coached while competing, even on the handball court. "Nice effort, Ken LaVigne. Stay in the middle of the court. Try to use the left hand more. You're vulnerable to that side." He also spoke differently than other coaches. There was a unique combination of formality and sincerity in his words and his voice. It's so very difficult to explain. He had a calming, reassuring effect on all of us.

Coach South was clever and very funny at times...without really trying to be funny. At one of our first practices at Rio Hondo, we were doing drills on the blocking sled. There was a player from a local school, Jesse, who was tough and physical but totally out of control. During a practice drill, we were to shuffle down the sled, striking each bag with a crisp but controlled punch. As always, Coach South stood behind us, making specific comments about our technique, "Short step. Quick hands. Drop your hips. Keep your head up. Step as you punch up! Stay in control." We each went through the drill, refining our technique as we progressed. Then came Jesse. He was totally out of control, hitting each bag wildly as he grunted and screamed. Halfway down the sled, he hit the bag so hard that it slid off the metal base it rested on and it flew into the air. The force of his hit threw him so far out of control that he staggered backward, laughing, screaming, and cussing as he regained his balance. It was a weird deal, and we all turned around to see Coach South's reaction. With his deadpan expression, he simply said, "That's all right, Jesse. Just keep working like that and we'll go out and spit on some cars after practice." We laughed, but Jesse actually thought that Coach

South was serious and snorted, "That'll be great!" Coach South simply shook his head and continued the drill.

Coach South said things that you wouldn't expect a coach to say; yet, his words always had great meaning. During a film session after a less than exemplary game, he stopped the projector, slowly walked up to the screen, and pointed at one of his linemen who had really fought to maintain his block, showing the type of desire Coach South wanted from all of us. "Gentlemen, this is an example of character. That character is inherent. Understand something. You don't develop character on a football field. You exhibit it." His voice was calm, but his message was clear. What he wanted was our effort. Nothing less. Nothing more. When he saw an upcoming opponent on film that was slow or lethargic, he would say something like, "It appears that this young man's lateral movement is less than impressive." He sounded more like a professor than a coach. That's what made him so extraordinary.

Coach South has remained a special person my life and the lives of many, many of his former players. He taught us football, but something much more important. He presented us with the best examples of character and integrity that I have ever heard or seen. He is the finest human being that I have ever known.

I learned a lot of important things from him, lessons that helped at the time and shaped me as a teacher and coach later in life. I learned that I didn't need to yell or cuss to be strong; in fact, doing those things only diminishes the respect that players have for their coach. He taught me to control my emotions and to treat others with humble respect. Most importantly, he taught me that true power comes from compassion and decency, not from authority, a title, or fame. He taught me what it truly took to be a man of character, dignity, and strength.

17

PERSPECTIVE

*"We often need to lose sight of our priorities
in order to see them."*

~ John Irving

LOUIE AND HENRY

Louie had been a varsity football player for La Serna during my last season as head coach. He was very talented, the only sophomore on the team, and had developed to be the best player at La Serna and in the entire area by the time he was a senior. He was everything a coach would want a player to be: strong, fast, smart, athletic, tough, unselfish, and extremely dedicated. At 6'0" and 205 pounds, he was not the biggest fullback and linebacker out there, but he was definitely the best. He was handsome, humble, and the most popular boy in school. He was normally serious but could be playful, too, and was selected by his teammates as the captain of the varsity team before his senior season. It was a great choice because, given all his skills and attributes, his best trait was that he was a great natural

90

leader. I really didn't know anyone who didn't like and respect him, so I was very excited when he decided to volunteer as an academic mentor in our OASIS program.

Henry entered OASIS as a sophomore who had failed most of his classes the previous year. He was a typical looking fifteen-year-old (if there is such a thing), thin with bushy brown hair that was slightly sun-bleached and draped over his face that was punctuated by an engaging smile. He loved to skateboard and hated schoolwork, making him a perfect fit for our program. Henry was friendly and didn't have the angry attitude of many of his classmates in our program, but he had a tendency to be two things that caused him most of his problems; he was lazy and moody. The biggest temptation in working with someone like Henry is to assume that his laziness and moodiness were choices on his part, things over which he had complete control. I fell victim to this temptation many times, making me a not-so-good teacher on several occasions. What I didn't fully realize until Henry's senior year was that, for the most part, he was conditioned to be these things by his life's circumstances.

Louie became Henry's mentor, and his influence was immediate and obvious. Henry looked up to Louie and would try to do what his mentor instructed him to do and was generally successful until the inevitable stumbling block twins, Moody and Lazy, periodically appeared. Henry would retreat into his own private world with his head resting on his folded arms across the table in front of him. At times, Louie could coax Henry out of his funk, but there were times that, despite Louie's best and most persistent efforts, Henry remained isolated in his self-made tortoise shell, resting his shoulders and head in a sort of classroom peekaboo.

That's exactly what happened one eventful Friday morning in November. Henry didn't feel like working. He was sleepy and just checked out, retreating to his happy, restful hiding place in his own arms. This time, however, Louie would have none of it. From my desk in the front of the room, I watched as Louie first whispered in Henry's ear, then spoke louder as he shook his arm, trying to get him to sit up and get to work. There was a big assignment due later in the day in Henry's World Civilization class, and he was teetering between a D and an F in the class. Louie never lost control of his temper, but it was easy to see that he was not giving up. He continued to talk, jiggle Henry's arm, and push the book under his shoulders, trying to break the trance of his self-absorbed at-risk mentee. Finally, Henry sat up with grumpy, sleepy eyes and scowled at Louie while telling him, "I just don't care. I'm not doin' it!"

This went on for five to ten more minutes before the bell rang, signaling lunchtime. Henry got up to leave, and Louie stood in his path. "You're not going anywhere until we finish this assignment!" Louie commanded. Louie's remark only increased the intensity of Henry's whining and insistence that he was just not going to do the work.

"Then I'm just gonna sit here with you until you change your mind," insisted Louie.

That was all I could take, so I walked up to them as everyone else filed out of the classroom except for the small group of students who always stayed, spending lunch to work on computers, chat, and finish assignments. There was something that Henry didn't know, something that made Louie's efforts to help his student the finest example of leadership I have ever witnessed from a student.

It was Friday, and the previous night, Louie and his varsity teammates played the tenth and final game of the regular season against defending league champion Santa Fe. La Serna had entered that game with a perfect 9-0 record with the hope of beating Santa Fe and winning a league championship for the first time in many years. It was a close game and wasn't decided until the very end when Santa Fe scored and destroyed the dreams of La Serna's varsity players, including their captain Louie. The kids were terribly disappointed and hurt by this loss. Even though their coach, as usual, insisted that they all attend school the next day and focus on their studies, no one blamed the many players who were too heartbroken to follow his orders and come to school.

Even though he was crushed by the loss, Louie attended school the next day specifically to make sure that Henry completed this assignment and not fall to an F grade in the class. He had the perspective and character to put aside his own heartache to help Henry pass a class he desperately needed to pass. The irony was that he was acting more like a champion than any high school athlete I had ever seen.

I approached their table. (I use tables and chairs in my classroom because it is more conducive to the support our mentors give their mentees.) I didn't wait to get there before speaking loudly and angrily at my selfish, ungrateful student. "Hey, you! Do you have any idea what you're doing? Do you realize what happened to your mentor and his team last night?" I explained the chronology of the past twenty-four hours and finished with, "This is ridiculous! Louie, I have always respected you but never more than I do now. Thank you for being the great person you are. Now, get out of here! Go have lunch with your friends. He doesn't deserve what you're giving him."

Then I wheeled on Henry, "Henry, I have never been this disappointed in a student in my life! Go on! Get out of here. Go sulk someplace else. You're honestly making me sick to my stomach!"

Louie repeatedly protested, telling me that it was all right, that he was going to stay until the work was completed. I was more stubborn than he was as I insisted, "This isn't a request, Louie. It's an order. Get the heck out of here! Thank you for inspiring me even if you didn't inspire the guy who should be the most grateful person on this campus."

Faced with my anger and insistence, Louie left while Henry just sat motionless in his seat, staring straight ahead. He stayed there for several minutes before I ordered him out of my room. I was fuming! He left but returned about ten minutes later with red, watery eyes that showed that he had been crying. "I want to finish my work," he said, standing in front of me.

"Then sit your butt down and get to it." I ordered.

Henry sat and worked for the rest of the lunch period. When the bell ending lunch rang, he walked up to my desk and told me that he was going to ask his teacher if he could finish the assignment after school and turn it in then. I didn't even look up when I answered, "Well, good luck." As soon as he left, I called his World Civilization teacher and briefly told her what happened, asking for the chance for Henry to come to my classroom after school to complete the assignment. She agreed, and sure enough, Henry reported to my classroom after school, skateboard in hand, and finished the assigned work, delivering it to his teacher who was spending after-school hours preparing for the Monday's lessons.

When he was leaving my classroom to make his delivery, I stopped him. "Henry, what you did today in class was wrong and selfish, but how you reacted tells me that you're the great kid I've always thought you were. I hope you take the time to thank Louie and apologize when you see him on Monday."

"You didn't need to tell me, Mr. LaVigne. I was going to do that anyway. I'm sorry for acting like a jerk." I just smiled and nodded at him as he left.

Henry never put his head down in class again. He was attentive and respectful to Louie every single day. He didn't fail any more classes, and two years later, I was floored when his senior English teacher told me something in mid-May of Henry's senior year. "Ken, I think there is something you need to know about Henry. He turned eighteen in December, and his parents threw him out of the house. He's been sleeping at friends' houses and a few times at a park since then but hasn't missed one single assignment on his senior project. He didn't want you to know, but I thought I just had to tell you." I later found out that Henry also never missed a practice or meet for our school's swim team that he had joined. I was in awe, and my mind went back to that pivotal day with Louie in my classroom.

I don't see my senior students every day but I try to touch base with them periodically, making sure that they are staying on track. I had spoken to Henry a few times after his parents kicked him out of his home, but he never let on that he had any such problem. I told him that I admired and loved him immensely, but I was disappointed that he didn't share his predicament with me so that I could have helped him. "Mr. LaVigne, you already helped me. You have enough to think about, and I knew I could take care of everything myself." I just shook my head and wiped my eyes. I really didn't know what else to say.

One of my most treasured memories as a teacher is of graduation day during Henry's senior year. My wife and I were getting out of our car when I spotted Henry in the parking lot all by himself about twenty yards away. He saw me at the same time and gave me a big smile. He also had a request. He had borrowed a shirt and tie for graduation from a friend but didn't know how to tie a tie. "Would you tie this for me, Mr. LaVigne?"

"Henry, I have never been more honored to do anything in my life." I gave him a Half-Windsor knot and adjusted it for him. As he started to walk toward his fellow graduates, I called out, "Henry, I'm very proud of you!" He smiled and then laughed as he turned to celebrate his remarkable journey with his friends.

18

INSPIRATION

*"Sometimes you wake up. Sometimes the fall kills you.
And sometimes, when you fall, you fly."*

~ Neil Gaiman

STEPHANIE

I have never had a student who inspired me more or touched my heart as deeply as Stephanie. Stephanie came to me later than her OASIS classmates, entering our program during the early fall of her junior year. Her counselor called me into her office and showed me the failing grades of this eleventh grader, asking if I could squeeze her into my English class and into our program. My answer was what it always is, "No problem! Send her to me."

While reviewing Stephanie's grades with her counselor, I noticed that her current English teacher was Dina Tsuyuki, our department chair and one of my closest friends. I thought it would be a good idea for me to get some insight about her from Dina, so I paid her a visit. Dina told me that Stephanie refused to do any work and was in a constant foul mood. I was concerned at this point because Dina is one of the finest teachers I know, and I had never heard of a student who didn't adore her and work hard for her. I realized that I would have my work cut out for me with this one.

The next day, Stephanie appeared in my room with a new class schedule, listing me as her third period English teacher. She just stood at the back of the room with a lost, angry look on her face and her schedule in her hand. I motioned for her to wait a few seconds while I got my other students started on some independent work. Then, I walked to the back of the room and asked her to come outside with me, "Step into my office, please."

We spoke briefly outside, and Stephanie's vacant look made a big impression on me. I was sizing her up, trying to make some quick judgment about the source of her problems in school. She was a tall, beautiful brunette with heavy makeup and revealing clothes. Her disinterest was obvious; yet, there was a softness, a vulnerability in her eyes that made me think that we had a chance to turn her around. I gave her the location of her assigned seat and promised that I would take it slow with her work in my class. Before ushering her back into the classroom, I made a plea, "Stephanie, I have no idea what's going on in your life that is stopping you from being a good student and happy person. Just please, please give me a chance to help you."

We came back into the classroom and I walked her to her seat, introducing her to the students sitting on both sides of her as well as to her mentor. It was normal for her to feel awkward and out of place in her new surroundings, so I didn't stress too much about her rigid demeanor. She refused to even look at anyone else, and I wondered what in the world was causing her to be so distant and disconnected. In time, I learned that it was amazing that she was even coming to school at all.

The casual atmosphere of our class and the genuine kindness from classmates and her mentor started to make a dent with her. She became friendly and even smiled from time to time. Weeks passed, and I was encouraged by the fact that she was attending school every day and was turning in work, good work that showed that she was paying attention. Because she was a member of our OASIS program, we monitored her grades in her other classes as well. She slowly started doing better and then one day, she came to talk to me.

"Mr. LaVigne, I heard that a lot of students spend lunch in here with you. Is it okay if I come in here, too?"

"Of course!" I told her. "We'd love to have you join us. Come in any time you want."

That same day, Stephanie showed up for lunch with a plastic bag carrying a Tupperware container with food. She asked if it was okay for her to use the microwave. "No problem. That's what it's there for." She warmed up her food and sat in the back of the room alone, eating. It wasn't long before one, then two, then more kids joined her, asking questions and just talking. It was nice to see her smile and laugh with her new friends, feeling more and more comfortable in her new safe place. As the days progressed, Stephanie began sitting at different tables, making new friends and making her way to the front of the room. One day, she sat at the table directly in front of my desk and asked me to try some of her homemade lasagna.

"Mr. LaVigne, you gotta try some of my lasagna. I made it myself from scratch. I brought extra for you. Try it!"

"Well, Stephanie, it sure looks good! I'll make you a deal. I make a pretty mean turkey sandwich. I'll have some of your lasagna if you'll split my sandwich with me. I can't eat both, so you'll do me a big favor if you share with me, too."

She agreed, and we sat together, sharing food and chatting. We laughed about little things that happened in school and the things we heard about in the news. She and the experience of seeing her open up were delightful. Then one day, she asked me to help her with an assignment that she didn't quite understand, so we sat together, figuring it out. This added dimension of our relationship made her even more relaxed and happy. Her grades started improving dramatically, and I would constantly tell her how impressed I was with her improved grades and wonderful personality. Then one day, she asked me a question.

"Mr. LaVigne, why do you do this? I mean, what do you get out of it."

"What do you mean, Stephanie? Why do I do what?"

"You know! Work with all these problem kids. You stay here at lunch and give everyone Cup-of Noodles and cookies. You're so nice to us! What do YOU get out of it?"

"I get to spend time with great kids like you. That's what I get from it."

She looked at me perplexed, but I also sensed that there was something else.

"No. I mean … you work with all of us who have all these problems. Why do you do that?"

"Stephanie, let me tell you something. I do it because I love you guys but also because, when I was your age, I was pretty screwed up myself. I had some very special people spend time with me and straighten me out. I guess that's the biggest reason. It meant a lot to me, and I hope it means a lot to you, too."

"It does," she said, looking sad and deep in thought.

I felt that this was a crossroads moment, so I asked her, "So what troubles you? What's happened to you that made you back away from everyone?"

That opened the floodgates, and Stephanie told me her story. She lived with her grandparents because her real parents were "complete wrecks". She almost never saw her father because he was always in jail. Her mother was a meth addict and still lived with her and her grandparents but was so strung out that she wasn't really a mother at all. Her grandparents still hoped for their daughter's, Stephanie's mother's, turnaround, but it never came. She just opened up, sharing stories of fear, neglect, and confusion. Then she dropped the big bomb on me. "And then there's my brother," she said with her eyes dropping to the table.

"I didn't know you had a brother. What's the story with him?"

She then shared that when she was thirteen-years-old, her brother started to sexually molest her, forcing her to do unspeakable things. She told me that she was scared to death and didn't say anything about it for a long time. When she finally found the courage to tell her mother about it, her mom first refused to believe her but eventually accepted that it had happened and continued to happen, but she minimalized it, saying that it was just a mistake and she should forgive her brother. Stephanie had come to her mother, wanting and expecting her to protect her from this abuse, and all she received was denial and indifference. That shattered her, and the abuse continued until she finally told her grandfather, who investigated, eventually kicking her older brother out of the house. That was it! No punishment for her brother! Her grandparents arranged counseling for Stephanie, but she felt that the people she loved and trusted the most had let her down.

She sadly told me, "It would've been great if I had a father who would have protected me." She grew silent and deeply sad after saying this.

"Well, I'll tell you something. As far as I'm concerned, I'm your dad, and I'll be proud to watch over you. Has your brother ever come back to hurt you? Are you in any danger now?"

"No. My grandpa threatened to go to the police, so my brother stays away now. The problem is just in my head and I get so depressed!"

"Are you getting counseling?" I asked.

"Yeah, but it doesn't help as much as I wish it would. I just get so sad or sometimes, I get so mad at everyone and everything!"

"You're on the right road now, kid. You have to promise me that you will let me know if you're ever in danger. I will make sure we do all we can to keep you safe."

Stephanie agreed and gave me a little smile. After school that day, I went to see her guidance counselor, telling her everything I learned. The counselor followed up, making sure that she was safe in her home and was receiving the counseling she desperately needed. I kept a close eye on her and our lunchtime visits continued throughout that year and into the next, her senior year. Stephanie blossomed into a lively, friendly, and generally happy kid with periodic moments of deep sadness and confusion. Her grades soared, and she began earning all A's and B's on her report cards. She was so proud of herself!

After her junior year, she asked me if she could be a mentor herself when she was a senior. Having OASIS students become mentors is fairly common, and I was delighted to have Stephanie join our mentor group, working with other at-risk students. She did a fantastic job, helping several classmates through their own dark periods. She was an absolute joy... and she made some great dishes to share with me during lunch while all I could offer her were my dumb sandwiches. She never seemed to care. It was the fellowship that filled both of our hearts.

Stephanie graduated the same year as Mark, my younger son. I was so proud of her for all she had overcome, and I told her so many times. These compliments always seemed to brighten her already beautiful face, giving her the validation that was denied her by those closest to her except her grandparents who were dedicated guardians for her. On the night of graduation, I was standing in a large group of graduates, friends, and parents basking in my own son's great accomplishments. As I stood in this throng of joy and pride, I saw Stephanie standing about five feet from me. She was crying. I went to her and asked her what was making her cry. She then gave me the greatest honor any teacher could ever ask for.

"What's the matter, Stephanie? Why are you so sad? This is a proud moment for you! You should be happy."

She turned slowly to me, and with tears streaming down her face, she said, "I wish you were my father."

I immediately felt that grasp of emotion that consumes me from time to time. "Stephanie, I am your father, and you're my magnificent little girl. I've told you that. I love you and I'm so very proud of you!"

She wrapped her arms around me tightly and struggled through the words, "Can I call you Daddy?" I just melted right there with tears now pouring out of my eyes. "I will always be honored to have you call me Daddy. I love you, kid!" She held on tightly for a few more minutes and walked away, but not before telling me, "I love you, Daddy," and then she was gone. I can teach for fifty more years and never hear more beautiful words than these from a student.

I kept in touch with Stephanie after she graduated. We made periodic calls to each other to see how we each were. She would occasionally stop by at lunch with burgers and French fries for us to eat. She remained the sweet, wonderful, caring kid she always had been, but she seemed to become increasingly aimless and lost. I talked to her about going to college and even made contacts with places and people where she could find a job. I wanted so desperately for her to find her way. She never did. I tried talking her through problems that I knew that she was having but I didn't see her every day, and that lack of support and encouragement finally made her succumb to the same circumstances that placed her in my class years earlier.

A few years after she graduated, I received a phone call from her sister. Stephanie was dead. Her grandparents found her in her bed in the morning. Stephanie had overdosed on drugs. I learned that, despite all her assurances to me that she was staying on the "straight and narrow" path, she had a boyfriend that was older than I was. He was giving her all the attention that she craved but for all the wrong reasons. He took advantage of her sexually in sickening ways I can't bring myself to think of let alone record in this account. He also was a constant and encouraging supplier of drugs for her, drugs that numbed her pain but also numbed her judgment. She desperately needed love and attention and thought she was getting it from someone who was simply taking advantage of her.

I attended her funeral with my wife and son. At the gravesite, the minister overseeing the service finished with what he was saying and then asked if anyone wanted to say a few words about Stephanie. I paused initially because I was so emotional and also because I did not want to preempt family members who wanted to speak. After a long, awkward, sad period of silence, it was obvious that none of them was going to say a word about this angel with her huge heart and deep sense of kindness. It was then that I spoke up and said how wonderful she was, how much I cared about her, and how grateful I was to have been her teacher. The only other two people who spoke on her behalf that day were her OASIS mentor and a classmate. It was so terribly unjust and disappointing. I am sure that her heart gave her a direct path to Heaven. I hope she knows how deeply she touched my life.

Stephanie became the inspiration for a new dimension of our OASIS program that continues to work with our students after graduation, giving guidance, support, and real life skills on how to enroll in college, apply for a job, write a resume, and interview. The growth, sense of direction, and self-confidence in these older students from our program motivate and inspire me but not nearly as much as my dear angel Stephanie, the sweet girl with a huge heart who I would have proudly had as my real daughter.

19

SELF-DISCIPLINE

"No person is free
who is not master of himself."

~ Epictetus

EDWIN

The first time I saw Edwin was during the summer before his freshman year in high school. He was one of the incoming freshmen who had some serious problems as a middle school student, failing classes and creating havoc in his teachers' classrooms. Because of this, he was placed in our Summer Bridge program, where he was grouped with other incoming freshmen, some also with problems and some who were outstanding students but participated in the program to get a head start in high school. He wasn't one of my students that summer, a fact for which I often thanked God as I observed him in combined activities with other teachers. This first observation was both startling and telling.

We had periodic field trips to local places—restaurants, arcades, city library, and the local bowling alley—to create a sense of cohesion among students and reinforce appropriate behavior. On this morning, students reported to the bowling alley where all of our classes would fill the place and spend some fun time together, building relationships with each other and teachers. Because I would be walking students back to campus after our excursion, I walked to the bowling alley so I wouldn't have to get a ride to my car after escorting kids back to campus when we finished bowling. Some students walked there, too, and some were dropped-off by their parents. Edwin was one of those whose parents dropped them off. He also had a few friends with him in the car, catching a ride from Edwin's mother. I was just entering the parking lot when I heard some unbelievable language being yelled by Edwin as he exited his mom's car.

"Don't fuckin' worry about it!' he screamed at his mother as his friends disembarked. "I don't give a shit what you want. I'll get home when I'm ready to get home. Just get off my fuckin' back!"

I was stunned at what I was hearing but was too far away to address him or his mother before she skidded out of the parking lot. His teacher walked up to him and it was obvious that she was chewing him out for cursing and talking to his mother like that. I thought to myself, "Thank God he's not one of mine!" but I knew that if he didn't undergo a miraculous transformation, it was only a matter of time before he would end up with me.

Edwin was a big kid, especially as a freshman. His appearance was menacing to his classmates and, truth be told, to many teachers as well. He was about 5'10" tall and looked like he weighed about 220 pounds. He had dark, curly hair that looked more like it had been scratched than combed. The stubble on his face revealed that he was already shaving but had neglected that chore for several days. He wore baggy clothes and had an arrogant smirk on his face at all times. He was a real piece of work! He was in the same class as my son Mark, and every day, I would hear stories about Edwin's acts of disrespect, vulgarity, and intimidation of other students. It was a good thing for Edwin and me that he never tried to bully or intimidate Mark. I have a fierce sense of protectiveness when it comes to my wife and sons, and God help anyone who comes close to putting them in harm's way. Luckily, I never had to address that situation.

I knew about Edwin because I had his older brother Dominic as a student. Dominic was a tough, edgy kid, but he was also a good-hearted soul. He was with me because he had a short fuse and refused to do schoolwork. Other than that, he was a model student. Dominic eventually failed his way out of OASIS and La Serna, choosing instead to go to continuation school where he would have more freedom. That freedom didn't get him very far, though, and he would come back to visit me, telling me that he hoped I would eventually work with Edwin. I never told Dominic, but when he said this, I always thought, "Not if there's a merciful God!"

Watching and hearing about Edwin during that first summer led me to the firm belief that he would not make it past his freshman year. His teacher that summer is one of the kindest, most caring, nurturing people I have ever encountered. Hearing about the disrespect that Edwin showed to her actually pissed me off, but I refrained from sticking my nose into someone else's business. Within a year, though, it became my business.

When I looked at my role sheets for the next fall, it was no huge surprise that Edwin's name was included. I knew immediately that we would butt heads (figuratively, of course) but also felt that maybe, just maybe, I could get through to him. We started the school year with him maintaining his macho bravado and arrogant sneers. I knew that openly confronting him would only polarize us, so I took a different approach. I would take him outside my class and have little chats with him, telling him that I sensed greatness and, yes, kindness in him. I would tell him that it just needed to get out, but I wasn't sure how to do it. I'd leave off by asking him to trust me and be patient with me. I also thanked him for listening to me and trying hard in class (something he really wasn't doing at the time, but I at least got him thinking about it). Basically, I was disarming him with humility. I also knew that patience would be a major key to his success.

In my classes, we focus on a different core value each week, defining, describing, discussing, and hopefully, applying them in our daily interactions. As with all my students, Edwin's initial and most recurring lessons involved these values and principles more that academic subject matter. He became immersed in discussions about empathy, compassion, integrity, and humility. I would praise him and other students whenever I noticed them exhibiting these principles. I truly believe that he thought I was crazy at first; many of my students do, but I felt that he was, for the first time in his life, finding his moral compass. We avoided the notion of absolutes, but affirmed the existence and importance of clear and definitive choices that make us all better human beings. He seemed to like these discussions, and his behavior and grades improved.

There continued to be many episodes of anger, disrespect, and defiance with Edwin, but through time, they became fewer and fewer. I would talk to his teachers, expressing my strong hope that we could save this kid. When discussing him with his teachers, I called him "quirky" to give a less threatening aura than his occasional shocking behavior. That seemed to work somewhat well, and we actually laughed together at some things Edwin did in class. For example, during his senior year, his English teacher was Dina Tsuyuki, my dear friend. She told me that every single day, Edwin would enter her class the exact same way. He made sure that he was one of the last students to enter and then would kick the door open and yell at the top of his lungs, "Daddy's home!" She said that, at first, it scared the hell out of her, but it became a sort of "class thing" to see and hear him make his entrance every day. Hey, whatever works!

Edwin also shocked me on more than one occasion, saying or doing things that immediately elicited a "What the Hell?!" thought in my mind. One thing he would do occasionally (and I have no idea why he did it), during a silent reading or writing period, was to randomly scream out, "No, Daddy! Don't! Please, Daddy! No!" and then just silently return to whatever he was doing. When he did this the first time, it scared the living heebeegeebees out of me, and I brought him outside to see what the matter with him was. "Nothin'," he said,

"I just like saying that. It's pretty cool, huh!" That "What the Hell?!" thought once again repeated itself in my mind.

"Come on, Edwin! That's pretty weird. Are you afraid of your father? Do you need help?"

"No. I'm fine. Everything's okay." To him, it was just some unique thing he did to get a response. He sure was successful there. I talked to his counselor about this, asking her to also speak to him about possible problems at home. We both kept an eye on him for bruises or other marks that might reveal abuse, but they never appeared. Edwin's random "quirks" were simply part of this complicated young man's personality just as was his insistence that graffiti is a basic human right. He was certainly a character, but became a less threatening and more respectful, compassionate character as time went on.

He ended up graduating from La Serna and made sure that he was standing right behind me with his hand on my shoulder while I kneeled in front of him in the photograph I take every year of our graduating OASIS seniors. He had come a long way and made every step of that journey a memorable one.

20

TENACITY

"But paradise is locked and bolted....
We must make a journey around the world to see if a
back door has perhaps been left open."

~ Heinrich von Kleist

CARLOS

I was at my desk when the bell rang, taking roll on my computer. Class was starting as it always does, slowly with quiet chatter and laughter. When I finished clicking the last little box on the screen with my mouse, I looked up and saw him standing in the doorway.

It was Carlos, fully decked out in his U.S. Army uniform with a huge smile on his face. He didn't look much different than he did five years earlier when I first met him as one of my new students. His grin widened as he just stood there for a minute, staring at me. I had another one of those full-body spasms that meant I was about to get too, too emotional. As he walked toward me at the front of the class, I just "lost it'" and began to cry. It's embarrassing as Hell when I get like that, and over the years, I've learned little techniques to feign getting something out of my eye or wiping my forehead as I slyly slide a paper towel across my eyes to hide the tears. There was no use faking it this time. I began to melt inside.

My students noticed that there was something wrong with me, not realizing that it was something totally opposite. There was something right with me, and I felt it to my core. They noticed this handsome Latin young man approach, slender, muscular, and filled with pride. They grew silent as Carlos reached my desk and gave me a hug that must have lasted for over a minute. "My God, I'm glad to see you," I told him as we stood there in front of my curious and somewhat embarrassed students.

"I said I'd be back," he replied quietly.

I introduced him to my students, "This is Carlos, one of my first OASIS kids. He's a great person and I'm glad you get to meet him." They continued to stare at us until I asked Carlos for a couple of minutes to get them started on an assignment.

"I did it," he said as we sat down to reconnect.

"You sure did! You look great in that uniform. Tell me how you've been."

Carlos started telling me about some of the things he had confronted and conquered since we last saw each other, and my mind slipped back to the time he was my student, sitting in the back row of the class, joking with me and giving me a hard time about anything and everything. He used to roll his eyes when I started another story about my coaching days, trying to illustrate some principle we were discussing in class. "Oh, no!" He'd say loud enough for everyone to hear, "Not another football story! You're not coaching anymore. Let it go, Mr. LaVigne," he'd say, giving me a smile and an exaggerated look of boredom. To be honest, he made me a bit crazy at times when he messed with me, but I couldn't get angry at him. He was too personable, too good-natured for me to stay frustrated.

When he'd get too playful in class or got off track, I'd call him on it, "Okay, Carlos, get to work."

"Why you pickin' on me? It's because I'm Mexican, isn't it?" Faking an incredulous expression.

"Of course, Carlos, if you were an Aryan brother like everyone else here, I would let you do whatever you want," I'd reply, thinking I was pretty clever myself as my 90 percent Hispanic students looked on.

"It's okay, Mr. LaVigne. I'm filled with compassion and empathy, so I'm able to forgive you." His wit and self-confidence were just too strong for me to verbally spar with him. I'd just shake my head and smile as I moved to the next subject, deferring to his mental and verbal prowess.

Carlos joined us with a litany of issues that kids his age should never have to endure. His father died of hepatitis when he was eight-years-old. Not long after that, his mother gave him up to relatives, choosing not to be a part of his life anymore. Carlos was shuttled from reluctant aunt to grandparent, never getting the stability or unconditional love that a kid that age desperately needs. This continued until he finally found a more secure home with his not much older sister and her husband who tried hard to settle his insecure spirit. That's when I met him and tried to give him that stability in school. It worked for a while, a long while as Carlos improved his grades and attendance, becoming one of our biggest success stories.

He continued his success story into his junior year, but the added burden of caring for an adolescent brother eventually proved to be too much for his sister in her early twenties. The bubble burst during that junior year, and he was shuffled to a more willing caretaker, his grandmother who lived in Montebello, a place too far for Carlos to stay at La Serna.

Carlos left our school with a 3.5 grade point average and a ton of self-confidence and tenacity. He was smart and had a plan. He was going to graduate high school, join the army, and save his money while earning educational opportunities from the army so he could go to college.

When he left, it was a sad, heartbreaking farewell, but he told me, "I'll be back, and you'll be proud."

Now he sat next to me in his army uniform, looking every bit the strong, self-reliant young man that I had prayed so many times for him to become.

He stayed for a while, talking with me until my students became restless and it was apparent that I had to get back to work. He stood and gave me another much appreciated hug before giving me his parting remarks, "Thanks, Mr. LaVigne. This all meant everything to me. I'll be back again. Don't forget me."

He didn't have to say that last part. There was no way I could ever forget him even if I wanted to, and I most surely didn't want to. My students watched silently as he left the room and I pretended to wipe my face to hide the tears.

21

LEGACY

"Show the world you are not here to just pass through. Leave great footprints wherever you pass and be remembered for the change you initiated."

~ Israelmore Ayivor

DASH

Not all of my experiences with young people involve students who have struggled with grades, bad behavior, and terrible home lives. Some of them have been with kids who are model citizens from nurturing families. One of these kids was someone very close to me from the very beginning of his life. In fact, Dashiell is the only child of two of my closest friends in the world, Hans and Susan Verstegen. His father, Hans, is more like a brother to me than just a friend. We grew up together, beginning in the second grade. We went to grade school, junior high school, high school, and junior college together, playing sports and fighting with as well as against each other as we forged a friendship as strong as I can imagine. It was a blessing as well as a stroke of luck that Dash and his parents lived in La Serna's attendance area, leading him to my school's doorstep.

Dash was a shy freshman when he entered La Serna. He wasn't even sure that he wanted to play football, but his father enrolled him in summer weight training with the hope that his old friend might ease his son's transition from a small private middle school to a public high school. It was a joy to have Dash participate in our football program, and it didn't take long for us to see that he was not only a nice young man but also an athlete with great potential to be an outstanding football player. He had a natural decency about him and he worked extremely hard in the weight room and on the field. As that first summer together drew to a close, Dash emerged as a starter on the freshman football team.

His quiet, respectful demeanor remained intact, but he soon developed a tenacity that made him a standout player. He was a big kid, weighing almost 200 pounds as a freshman, unlike his father who was smaller as a running back in his days of playing football. Dash was certainly a lineman with big, strong legs and an increasingly muscular build. He pounded weights with his teammates and made steady improvements in his strength with a fierce competitive nature. He continued to grow, weighing close to 240 pounds with very little body fat as a senior. During the summer before his senior year, Dash was so intense during a workout that he went ballistic on a fellow starter whom he felt was loafing. He erupted in a confrontation in which he approached an equally large and strong lineman, challenging him to work harder. The other players in the weight room stood speechless as Dash openly said loud and clear what needed to be said to this loafing teammate. It needed to be addressed and Dash was the only one in the room with the courage to do it.

The others watched in frozen silence as Dash worked like a fearless surgeon, removing a tumor of laziness that threatened the health and life of his team. It took several players to hold him back before he literally attacked his slacking teammate. I was impressed with his intensity and devotion, but I brought him outside to express my concern for his loss of control. Dash understood and with uncommon maturity, sought out this other player and initiated a long conversation to clear the air. His self-control paid off for all of us because we went on to have a great season and go to the playoffs.

Even though he was fiercely competitive, Dash never lost his playful attitude. He would often say or do something that made us all smile or laugh during practice, in a team meeting, or in the classroom. He was a student in my junior English class, and I still remember walking up behind him in class one day as he drew a comic strip of the hero, "Dashman" with a cape, mask, and magic stick. As I stood behind him, he looked up at me and instead of being worried about being caught messing around in class when he was supposed to be writing a paper, he just looked up at me and grinned, saying, "Pretty cool, huh, Coach?" It was impossible to get mad at him, so I just said, "Yeah, Dash. Very cool! Now, let's finish the assignment. Okay?" He told me that he just had a couple more finishing touches on his cartoon masterpiece, and then he would complete the writing assignment. Normally, I would have told him to put that stuff away NOW, but the simple joy in his eyes disarmed me, so I just said, "Hurry up! You're killin' me, Dash!" as I took a deep breath and walked away.

It is amazing how much better I became as a teacher and coach after I became a parent. A new awareness in me grew as I wished, hoped, and dreamed for the best things possible for my own two sons. Suddenly, my students had new faces as precious treasures of their hopeful, adoring parents. That awareness was never more real than during the years I coached and taught Dash. Sure, he wasn't my son, but he was the closest thing possible. I saw him as a vulnerable baby in the arms of his proud parents and my dearest friends. As a young child, I saw him play make-believe, pretending to be any number of cartoon heroes that he watched on Saturday mornings. I listened to his devoted father countless times, talking about a variety of concerns, proud moments, and childhood milestones. Eventually, I saw him develop into one of the finest football players I ever coached, earning well-deserved all-league, all-area, and All-CIF honors, distinguishing him as one of the best high school football players in Southern California. I saw both sides of that face that stared back at me through the bars of his facemask during practices and games, his and his parent's.

We had a tradition after our last varsity game each year in which I held all the seniors in the bus that returned us to school while the underclassmen all lined up in single-file outside the bus, waiting to give a final tribute to their senior teammates when they exited the bus and entered the locker room for the last time. While in the bus with my seniors, I would tell them all how much I love and respect them. I thanked them for all their dedication and loyalty, then, one by one, I tearfully hugged them and sent them out to make that last walk to the locker room. It is an extremely emotional experience that strangely fills and drains the heart at the same time. After Dash's last game, that goodbye to him was the most difficult, sad, and emotional farewell I have ever given in all my years of coaching.

The bus was dark as I stood in front of young men I dearly loved and would sorely miss. There was an added sadness and frustration in the hearts of my seniors because we had just lost in the second round of the playoffs to a team that we could have and probably should have beaten. Little mistakes cost us the game and abruptly ended the dreams of my departing warriors. There were sounds of heartbroken kids who had worked so hard to realize a dream that was now unattainable. I talked to all of them as a group before sending them out individually to take that final walk. Finally, it was time to say goodbye to Dash, and I just wasn't ready to do that.

He stood up slowly from his seat on the bus and walked to me with his head down. When he reached me, he slowly lifted his head and looked at me while sobbing uncontrollably. I felt my face contort in my own inconsolable sobs. I stared at him and remembered all the steps he had taken over the years. Visions of him giggling like a third grader after saying or doing something silly and of him snarling as he prepared for the challenge of a big game filled my head. We hugged in a rocking embrace with our hands clutching each other, me with his jersey locked in my fists and him with his hands clinging tightly to my shirt.

"I love you, Dash. I don't know what we're going to do without you! Thank you for everything."

"Oh, coach. I don't want to go!" he sobbed.

"I don't want you to go either, but it's time. You're headed for bigger and better things."

I didn't need to be a prophet to predict his future success. He has all the qualities of a winner: great character, a willingness to outwork everyone else, and a deep-rooted goodness that would not only serve him, but everyone around him. What I couldn't imagine at the time was that his journey would lead him back to La Serna as a teacher and coach where he continues to grace my days as I watch him spread his patient leadership, strength, and wisdom over the lives of his own students and players. His legacy as a player now extends to that of a coach. I am lucky and proud to have witnessed it.

Dashiell Verstegen was a student and football player at
La Serna High School and returned as a teacher and coach.

22

RELEVANCE

*"To bring relevance to people, you have to be able
to speak their language effectively"*

~ Sunday Adelaja

VENUS AND PATRICK

There are many reasons for our success in helping at-risk students rediscover themselves and achieve academic success. Teaching and reinforcing core values is the skeleton on which everything else is built. Establishing and maintaining as much parent involvement as possible is a crucial component, and nothing could ever be accomplished without the tremendous support of our district and school administrators, counselors, teachers, and clerical staff. There is one factor, however, that is the biggest key to the success of our program and our students. The dedicated leadership of our volunteer student academic mentors is, without doubt, the biggest reason that so many lives have been saved in OASIS. The relationships forged between mentors and students serve as the heartbeat of

118

everything we do in our collective effort to change attitudes, develop character, and create habits of success.

It's all about relationships and the powerful influence that they have that make the difference. Knowing that, we recruit and train the very best students in our school to serve as academic mentors to tutor, motivate, monitor, and lead students who never experienced that influence before. Most of our academic mentors are high-performing scholars, students who have the highest grade point averages and the most extensive extra-curricular involvement in the school, but that's not always the case. The most important characteristic that we seek in our mentors is, quite simply, a good heart. Mentors have to sincerely care about helping others and possess a relentless tenacity to continue giving support even when their assigned students ignore, disrespect, and, at times, verbally abuse them. They must be strong enough to know that, when the smoke clears and their journey with their at-risk partners is done, it will all work out. That takes courage and uncommon devotion.

Sometimes, our most effective mentors are those who have stumbled and needed help themselves in the past. These young people can relate to the struggles of those they are mentoring, and often, this relevance is what makes all the difference in the world. That was the case with Venus Fields, a two-year academic mentor who had known too well the feeling of failure upon failure before a door finally opened for her and she walked through. Venus is one of the most incredible kids I have ever met. Her personal story began as a "crack baby" who was taken away from her mother because there was simply no way that she would be able to raise a child. Venus lived with her aunt, a devoted guardian who worked hard to mold her niece into a healthy, happy, and successful child. That didn't always work as Venus grew up, displaying defiance and disrespect that is understandable for a child in her circumstances. Through her aunt's devotion and her own realization that the road she was taking would lead to nowhere, Venus straightened herself out, passing classes and becoming involved in school activities.

Venus was beautiful with an easy smile, gracing her ebony face that was dominated by her quick and engaging countenance. She was strong-willed with a "No, you didn't" reaction to those foolish enough to give her a hard time. She also had a huge heart that never let her give up on her students. She always asked for the most difficult students to mentor, so that's what I gave her. One of her early students was a "gang banger" who had just been let out of a juvenile detention center when she began working with him. His father had been murdered in prison just two months before he was introduced to Venus, and he was angry and out of control. That didn't dissuade Venus in the least. Her calm, strong demeanor was supplemented by her compassion and patience. I watched in awe as she worked with this young man, commanding his respect with her steady leadership. He would confront anyone else at the drop of a hat but would melt at her command to "just get over it and do something that shows you're really strong." She lost that kid because he had problems and needs beyond the scope of our abilities, but she never lost his trust and respect.

Another one of her assigned students was a boy named Patrick, a timid and disorganized mess of a student when she began working with him. He wasn't defiant or mean-spirited. He was just a car, driving down the road aimlessly without a steering wheel. Venus became that steering wheel and a lot of other things, too. She'd work tirelessly to make sure his notebook was organized, his assignments were written down, and his work was done. I'd chuckle when I'd see her give him one of her "Don't give me any of your lip" warnings before bearing down on him with a steady dose of hard work. She was inspiring to watch, and I soon came to respect and love her very much.

The foundation she laid with Patrick is the reason he graduated from high school. She guided him to better grades and disciplined work habits. She also instilled a work ethic in him that I don't think he would have received from any other mentor. That sense of responsibility and positive reaction to strong leadership proved to be critical for him at the end of his senior year.

Patrick was passing all of his classes but was having major problems completing the final steps in his senior project, a culminating experience we require of all our seniors that involves an extensive research paper, hours of fieldwork, and an oral presentation of their work in front of a panel of teachers and community members. Like many of our seniors, Patrick was overwhelmed by all the work he had to do and was not completing essential benchmarks. He was in serious danger of not graduating, and time was running out.

Knowing that he was one of my OASIS students, Dina Tsuyuki, his English teacher and my close friend, called me at home one evening in late April, telling me that she didn't think that Patrick was going to make it unless something miraculous happened. She asked me to talk with Patrick, and I was more than ready to do what she asked. I emailed his parents, explaining the situation and called Patrick at home. He answered the phone in his normal frightened voice.

"Patrick, this is Mr. LaVigne. Mrs. Tsuyuki just called me and told me that you haven't turned in your fieldwork time sheet, outline, and research paper for your senior project. She said that you won't graduate unless this is all turned in by Friday and that your class presentation is scheduled for Wednesday of next week. What's going on?"

He stammered and mumbled through what he thought was an explanation, but it really was evidence of his lack of preparation. He finished by telling me that he was going to talk to his mother in the morning and ask her to call relatives who were flying in from Hawaii to see his graduation to cancel their flight because he wasn't going to graduate. Venus's foundation of tough love allowed me to slide into my coach identity, speaking very loudly with a threatening tone.

"The Hell you will!" I blared. "You will NOT do that! What you will do is stay up all night for the next two days and get your work done! Then, you're gonna do your PowerPoint and make your presentation to the class next week on your scheduled day. Too many people have put too much time and effort into you for you to quit now. You will NOT quit. You will NOT let your parents or yourself down! I'm gonna tell you something, Patrick. You will take care of all of this or I promise that horrible things are going to happen to you! I want to see you in my room at 7:30 AM sharp every day for the next week. You're gonna show me what you've done, and you sure as Hell better not let me down! Do you understand?"

A soft voice answered, "Yes, Mr. LaVigne. I understand. I'll be there and I'll get it done."

"Make sure you do or I'll hunt you down! Got it?"

"Yes sir! I got it."

I'm sure that I wasn't very professional in my phone conversation with Patrick that night and my threats of "horrible things" happening to him and my promise to "hunt him down" likely sounded more like a horror movie than a conversation with a teacher, but it was an example of my determination to do whatever it takes to get him past that finish line. It worked! Patrick came to see me every morning and completed all of his work. He made his senior project presentation to his panel of judges, and I heard that it was one of the best they had ever seen. Patrick's relatives kept their plane reservations and made the trip to watch him walk across the stage and receive his diploma. None of this would have ever been possible without Venus, his amazing and devoted mentor.

When Venus was a senior, she listened intently to my answer to a question by one of the students in class, "Mr. LaVigne, when are you going to retire?" I responded by telling all my students that I was not going to retire until I made sure that there was someone who cared as much as I did to continue our program. After class, Venus stayed behind because she wanted to tell me something. She asked if I was serious about what I told the class about not retiring until I found the right person to take over. When I told her that I was completely serious, she told me that she wanted to be that person. She wanted to teach and be the next director of OASIS.

"I couldn't hope for a better person to do it, Venus. Go to college, get your degree, and complete your teaching credential. I'll wait for you, but don't take too long. I'm getting kinda old," I said with a proud and hopeful smile. I am waiting, waiting for just the right person, and there is no one more right than Venus.

23

PATIENCE

"Trees that are slow to grow bear the best fruit."

~ Molière

JOHANNA

An incredible mentor in our program was a petite and beautiful girl named Johannah. She was an outstanding student, one of our school's highest ranking scholars with a grade point average that most people would think is impossible to achieve. Her quiet nature concerned me at first. I wondered if she would be able to stand up to who would most likely be tough, aggressive students to mentor. My concerns were quickly erased as I saw her work with her two assigned students, Sara and Maria.

Johannah was a serious student and a genuine example of patience and compassion. She was a devout Christian but never once spoke about her faith or religion. She simply showed others, through her example, what a good soul should be. She attentively worked with both girls every day, sitting in the back row while bouncing from one student to the next, helping them with their work. She was kind but demanding. She expected her students to try, and when they didn't try, she would come to me and ask for permission to work with Sara and Maria during lunch so that they would complete their assignments. She was a tough mentor, but a loving and nurturing one as well.

Johannah guided these two girls beyond where they thought they could go, patiently explaining social studies projects and walking them through algebra equations. Her beautiful, tiny face would squint with disapproval whenever either girl seemed disinterested or lethargic. She would show them how to do something and insist that they demonstrate their understanding by completing another math problem or science question on their own. She did all of this without ever berating or belittling them. It was obvious that she believed in them and her confidence rubbed off on them. Both girls steadily improved their grades and had near perfect attendance. When they did miss school, Johannah would call them from our classroom, delivering some of the best "guilt spears" I have ever heard. All her efforts led to positive habits and lives changed.

Johannah's sincere conviction became even more evident when she graduated. Being one of La Serna's best students, she was accepted to some of the finest universities in the country. She postponed her college career for a year to serve as a missionary in the Far East for her church. There was not a bit of phoniness in her; she was as true and genuine as anyone I've ever seen, and her impact on her students was life-changing.

24

CONFIDENCE

*"No one can make you feel inferior
without your consent."*

~ Eleanor Roosevelt

SARA

From the very first day, Sara was a character. Undeniably pretty, even without makeup or the fashionable clothes that her classmates wore, she sat in my class with a constantly bewildered look, looking around for clues from others about what her weird old teacher was trying to explain. She was wise in her understanding of others and compassionate in how she treated them unless she felt that they were being less than nice and respectful toward her. During those moments, she would turn to the transgressors and say in her deep raspy voice, "What are you looking at? You better watch out! Don't get me mad." That usually did the trick because her appearance left no doubt that she was all about being real and not phony or pretentious.

Sara came to school every day dressed in her usual uniform: grey baggy sweatpants, oversized tee shirt, tennis shoes, and no makeup. She acted like she really didn't care what others thought of her even though, deep down, she did. Her kind spirit and fun personality made her popular with her classmates who loved to spend time talking with her during class or lunchtime when she took up regular residence in my classroom. She was also a caring, unselfish young girl who would do anything to help others or show her love and appreciation for them. During a field trip to the Aquarium of the Pacific, she surprised me with a cute stuffed tortoise, giving it to me as I sat with a couple counselors who accompanied us for the day.

"Mr. LaVigne, this is for you," she said as she held it out for me. "It reminds me of you," she said softly in her raspy, adorable voice. I got a big kick out of both her generous gesture as well as the fact that it was a tortoise. I keep my hair cut in an almost shaved crew cut because of a few reasons. First, I am almost bald, and my hair, when allowed to grow, makes me look a bit like Father Junipero Serra, the missionary who made a lasting imprint in early California history. I also liked my hair very short because it was easier to get dressed in the morning without having to worry about an unavoidable bad hair day. Lastly, my wife says she likes it that way, calling me her "little turtle" because I actually look like a turtle with my round, bald head.

I couldn't wait to get home and have a few laughs with Gisele after I shared Sara's comment about the tortoise reminding her of me. It was not unusual for Sara to present gifts to others even though her family did not have the resources for non-essential goods. She simply had a heart of gold.

What Sara didn't have was confidence in her abilities as a student. She saw things simply without complicated nuances and details. Johannah, her mentor, worked hard with Sara, developing an understanding of basic concepts and implementing good work habits. This helped Sara greatly, but couldn't eliminate her tendency to see things in a singular perspective. Details and multi-tasking drove Sara crazy, and periodically, she would listen to my extended lessons and participate in assigned activities until she finally had enough and voice her frustration to me in front of the class, "Enough of this, Mr. LaVigne. Just say it. What's your point, anyway? Stop all this mumbo jumbo and just get to your point!"

Her frustrated pleas for simplicity never failed to endear her to me even more than she already was, "Okay, Sara, the point is……" And then I would summarize the key idea that I thought I was so creatively illustrating to my class. It was actually a great way to end these lessons, leading Sara to exclaim in her raspy voice, "Then why didn't you just say that and not put us through all this other crazy stuff?" I'd smile and we'd move on.

Sara's desire to cut to the chase was never more evident that during her junior year when she was a student in my English class. She was doing a good job, not a great job but a good job, in her classes, but was struggling with a big research project we were working on. The project focused on the Bill of Rights and involved the application of those rights to contemporary social issues. Students had to research an issue in American society and write a paper on how that issue was impacted by the rights guaranteed to all American citizens and then give an oral presentation, stating a clear thesis. Sara chose airport security searches and their relationship to Americans' right to privacy. It was an ambitious choice, and I was impressed with her willingness to address the issue.

Sara fell squarely on the side of security, feeling that the threat of terrorist bombing on jetliners was a reasonable situation that required citizens to forfeit some of their rights to privacy. She wrote a pretty darn good research paper but was having difficulty preparing her oral presentation. Part of my instruction involved the use of a prop, an object that would symbolize the essence of her argument. That threw her for a loop until we discussed it, and she decided to use a baby blanket as her prop that would be introduced at the beginning of her presentation and reintroduced at the very end. Her point was that when we are babies, we think we can avoid danger by simply hiding underneath our baby blanket, but as adults, we know that it takes a lot more than a blanket to keep us safe. It was a great choice as a symbolic prop, and we worked on it together until it was time for her presentation.

A part of this process was dressing appropriately for the presentation. Males were expected to wear a shirt and tie (I kept several extras in my classroom for the boys who didn't own them). Females were expected to wear nice slacks and top or an appropriate dress, one that was semi-formal and businesslike. I worried about this part because none of us had ever seen Sara wearing anything but sweatpants and a tee shirt. In the days leading up to her presentation, I reminded her of the requirement of appropriate attire.

Sara blew everyone's mind on the day of her presentation by coming to school in a nice dress and heels. She was gorgeous! She even wore makeup. She astonished us all even more when she got up in front of the class and with minimal use of any notes, gave a dynamic presentation that combined scholarly inquiry with "in your face" common language that only Sara could pull off.

"You see this baby blanket, man? Well, a baby uses it to cover up and hide from danger, but we're not little kids, damn it! We don't need no stupid blanket! We need safety and we gotta be checked before we get on a plane. Damn! I don't wanna get blown up! Do you?" That's how she started her presentation, following it with facts she learned doing research. She finished her speech by grabbing the blanket and telling us, "This blanket is stupid! Only little kids hide under blankets, and I'm not a dumb ass little kid. I want protection!"

Everybody was silent as she sweetly said, "Thank you for paying attention to me," as she walked back to her seat. The entire class erupted in applause. She nailed it! It wasn't polished or pretty, but it was powerful and impressive. All we could say was, "Wow! Great job, Sara!" She was so proud! She conquered both the assignment and her fear of public speaking. When she gave her senior project presentation the next year, everyone on her panel raved about her delivery and performance. Sara had blossomed into a confident, serious student, and we all celebrated her achievements with the praise that she had lived so long without. Seeing her graduate with that empowering confidence and joy of accomplishment was one of the best things I have ever witnessed.

25

DETERMINATION

"It had long since come to my attention that people of accomplishment rarely sat back and let things happen to them. They went out and happened to things."

~ Leonardo da Vinci

MARIA

M aria was also one of Johannah's students who grew as both a student and person under the tutelage of her caring mentor. Maria's growth, however, surpassed even our most ambitious expectations. She was a shy, quiet girl as a sophomore student in my class and responded well to Johannah's guidance. She was tiny and resembled a doll every bit as much as a sophomore student in high school. Her curly brown hair was always perfectly coifed, and although her clothes were not new or fancy, she always looked... well, she just looked cute as a bug.

Living with her mother and her mother's boyfriend in a small apartment in which Spanish was the only language spoken, Maria struggled through a home life of turmoil and financial difficulties. As time went on, though, Maria became more and more serious about school and her future. You'd never know it by simply speaking with her. She barely said more than two or three words at a time and spoke so softly that you had to really listen hard to hear and understand what she said. The true extent of her dedication to her studies happened during her senior year. She had become a mentor herself, helping younger students the way Johannah had once helped her. The biggest impression on all of our students occurred one morning during a presentation on graduation requirements by Shanna Moore-Garcia, a fantastic guidance counselor at La Serna.

During the first semester, I schedule a different person on our staff to come and talk to our OASIS sophomores every Wednesday about different important issues related to their success in school. Our principal, assistant principals, security officer, and counselors give outstanding presentations to our students, sharing stories and giving information on things that will help them be successful. Nobody did a better job than Shanna! She would talk to the students about things they should do and things they should avoid, but the main thrust of her presentation was a comprehensive review of our school's graduation requirements. At the end of her presentation, she would walk them through a checklist that they each made, listing every class they needed. She implored them to keep this checklist in their notebooks, not only during their sophomore year, but every year until they graduate.

Noticing a senior mentor in class with the sophomores, Shanna asked Maria if she remembered the presentation from her sophomore year. Maria simply smiled as she opened her binder, pulling that very sheet that she kept updated and in the front of her binder. Shanna and I were both wide-eyed as Maria waved it in the air and walked it over to us with all the classes checked off and notes in the margins. We were just blown away. Maria "got it" and had taken control of her own future. It was an amazing moment!

What was even more amazing occurred during the last month of the year. La Serna's first principal, Melvin Locke, has served as our school's leader for its first twenty-two years before retiring. He was the beloved patriarch of our school and our gymnasium was named after him. The first graduating class of La Serna respected him so much that they raised money every year and presented a $1,000.00 scholarship to an outstanding graduating senior. Students who were considered had to submit an application and were interviewed by a panel composed of this first graduating class. It was one of the most prestigious awards that anyone could possibly win at our school, and the finest students at La Serna applied for the honor and scholarship.

Maria had the initiative and confidence to apply for it as well, going head-to head against students who had been accepted to schools like Harvard, Stanford, and Dartmouth. She not only competed against these accomplished students, she won! Maria was selected as the recipient of the Melvin Locke Scholarship and in doing so, electrified all of our at-risk students. I spoke to one of our teachers who knew people on the interview panel, and he told me that after she told her story of perseverance and determination, several panel members actually cried. Hearing about this award and knowing Maria, so did I.

26

EMPATHY

*"I do not ask the wounded person how he feels,
I myself become the wounded person."*

~ Walt Whitman

ARMANDO

It's no great revelation to say that children, especially teenagers, do things that surprise us; but sometimes, their actions expose a depth of character that is so unpredictable and unexpected that it just takes your breath away. Months into the fall semester one year, some of my most challenging, seemingly incorrigible boys did something that completely changed my perception of them and changed the life of a fellow student they didn't even know.

Donny, Nick, Rodrigo, and Ron were sophomores who were in the midst of my initial onslaught of core value training, and to be honest, I had serious doubts that any of them were internalizing the principles of empathy, compassion, and responsibility that I was preaching in my classes. They would routinely arrive late to

132

class, clown around when they were supposed to be working, and poke fun at classmates even after it became apparent that their comments were unprovoked and, at times, hurtful. They seemed to have some deep-rooted feelings that homework was not part of their set of responsibilities and that their promises to improve could easily be forgotten. They weren't bad kids, just good kids who continually made bad choices.

Much of their apathy and irresponsibility was understandable. Rodrigo's father was serving a life sentence for murder, and his mother was a drug addict that relinquished full control of her son to yet another unprepared single grandparent who was given the job of raising a child forty years younger than her. Don's parents were both drug addicts with gang affiliation. His father was in prison, and his mother was a citizen of the streets, leaving Don to be raised by a reluctant aunt who struggled daily with the defiance of her unappreciative and rebellious nephew. Ron and Nick were just kids who thought that teenage life was all about partying and having fun and not about discipline and academic goals. They were all extremely likable, but also extremely unreliable.

One day during lunchtime, I hustled out of my classroom to go to the restroom, a daily practice necessitated by my room full of kids who found safety and acceptance on the other side of my door. I had just finished when the four of them rushed to me, disturbing their own routine of cruising the hallways. They had a sense of urgency that I had not seen in any of them before.

"Mr. LaVigne, there's a kid in trouble! Something's wrong!" One of them shouted as they ran toward me.

I thought someone was hurt or being attacked by other students, so I stopped and listened to their out-of-breath explanation of the problem. "There's a guy sitting on the hill next to your room with his head down, and we think he's crying. We asked him what was the matter, and he didn't even answer. There's something wrong!"

"Where is he?" I asked, trying to decipher where, exactly, this kid was. They led me to the area outside my classroom and pointed to the place just beyond a fence that was intended to be a barrier, keeping students away from a steep hill that bordered my classroom on the second story of our building. I moved quickly to where they led me but didn't see anyone. We all looked at each other with mystified expressions, and one of them said, "Well, he was here a minute ago. You gotta find him, Mr. LaVigne; there's definitely something wrong."

I looked over the fence, craning my neck to see around the corner of the bottom level of the building, but I still couldn't see him. I retraced my steps around the other side of the building and looked down into the quad in an attempt to locate someone who appeared to be isolated or showed uncommon sadness. It didn't take me long before I saw a small male student, sitting by himself with his face in his hands. I looked at my four guardian angels and asked if this was the boy they were talking about. "Yeah. That's him," one of them confirmed, so I walked down the stairs to talk to this mysterious boy in need.

I sat down next to him on a planter that also served as seating for students eating lunch or waiting for their next class. "Hey, buddy, are you alright?" I asked with no reply. "Man, look at me. You look really sad. Something must be wrong. What's going on?"

The boy slowly pulled his hands from his face and looked at me. He was crying, and his eyes had a desperate, frightened look that I have seen in too many other kids' faces.

"My name is Mr. LaVigne. I'm a teacher. My room's upstairs. I'm worried about you and I want to help you. What's going on? By the way, what's your name?"

"Armando. My name is Armando. I don't have any place to go. No one likes me. They make fun of me," he whimpered back.

"That's not true, Armando. You have place to go—my classroom. I have lots of kids in there who would love to have you join them. Really! I'm not kidding! Heck, I'd love it if you hung out in there. Honest!"

My words didn't have any huge effect on him except that they seemed to at least interrupt his tears. He turned his head toward me and just stared. I repeated my offer for him to come spend time in my room as the bell rang, ending lunch. I threw in one final question, "Do you have a class down here?"

He told me that his next class was German with Ms. Gerlach, a great teacher who was also luckily very caring and nurturing. "Okay," I said, "Talk to Ms. Gerlach and tell her that Mr. LaVigne talked to you. She'll let you know that I'm not some creepy, weird guy, and that you should take me up on my offer."

I raced back up to my classroom, and before the tardy bell rang, I quickly called Jennifer Gerlach and explained what had just happened. She told me that Armando was a nice kid but a bit of a loner. He tried hard but just didn't seem to click with the other students in her class. She promised to talk with him and keep a close eye on him, too. I asked her to please encourage Armando to come to my room when he doesn't have any place to go, and then I hung up the phone to start my class as the bell rung.

I began my class and gave the students and their mentors some things to do independently. After they began working, I grabbed my phone, dialed Armando's counselor, and faced the back corner of the room behind my desk to minimize what my students could hear in the conversation. I explained the situation to Armando's counselor and asked her to call him in to have a talk. That afternoon, I received a call from her, telling me that she had done what I asked. She confirmed what I instinctively knew. Armando was a timid kid with some undeveloped social skills that led others to either ignore him or make fun of him. She told him to seek me out and find my classroom. She assured him that he would feel comfortable there. I thanked her and hung up the phone as the noise level in the room revealed that independent work time was over. I had to get back to work.

The next morning, I was hopeful that Armando would muster the courage to come visit my classroom, but I didn't really expect it. It usually takes at least a few days before one of these "Cyphers in the Snow" takes the plunge and comes to visit. Dick Torres, my old coach and mentor, told me a long time before about a story he read about a boy who was left out alone in the snow, abandoned by everyone who could have and should have come to his rescue. That story had a powerful impact on me, especially because I heard it from someone as important in my life as Dick Torres. During the morning, Diego, Ron, Donny, and Nick each asked about this sad, lonely boy they found the previous day. I told each of what I had done and asked them to be especially kind to Armando if they saw him in my classroom or in the halls. They were genuinely worried about this kid they didn't even know, and I was moved by their caring interest.

I was surprised to look up from my desk during lunchtime and see Armando's frightened face appear in the slowly opening door to my classroom. "Armando, great to see you! Come on in! Want some cookies?" I said as he reluctantly completed his entrance into my room. He walked slowly to my desk, looking at the other students in the room as they sat in clusters, talking or working on the computers. When he finally made it to my desk, I opened up a drawer in the front cupboard and pulled out a cookie jar filled with sugary treats. "Take some," I said as I set the cookie jar on the table in front of the desk. "I like the chocolate chip ones the best. I'm on a constant diet, and they're my biggest temptations."

Armando carefully examined the contents of the jar and pulled out a few cookies. He stood in front of me and surveyed the class, finally asking the obvious, "Is this your classroom?"

"Yeah! What do you think of it? It's a pretty nice classroom, huh?" My classroom is pretty unconventional. I take a lot of pride in making it a visually inviting place. There are posters and photographs of students on all the walls. There is a full-sized refrigerator stocked with big bottles of spring water and a microwave on a front counter that is in perpetual use, warming up Cup-of-Noodles that we keep on hand for hungry little stomachs. A stereo is usually playing students' choice of music. My rule is as long as there is no cussing, especially "F Bombs", they can listen to whatever they want. There's a piñata, safari hat, Japanese figurines, and a real-looking statue of a pug dog that all have special meaning and memories as student gifts. Then there are the kids, students who are in small group conversations or in the midst of several conversations with others at the same time. It's a pretty lively place.

Earlier in the morning, I told my students that there might be a new kid who would stop by for a visit. I didn't go into details, but I did tell them that Armando was a nice kid who needed a place to feel safe and welcome. I asked them to be nice. What I witnessed in the room that day while Armando stood by my desk, sheepishly nibbling cookies, was beyond nice. It was downright inspiring. Several students noticed this new guy standing in front of me and put two and two together. They started coming up to Armando, asking his name and what classes he had.

Conversations expanded to include invitations to "come over here and sit with us". My incredible students introduced themselves as well as their friends. It was amazing to see Armando smile and hear his soft, shy voice talk to his newfound friends.

Armando became a regular in my classroom at morning break as well as lunch. Students with drug-addicted parents in jail reached out to him with genuine kindness. Kids who typically had surly personalities welcomed him every day and asked him how he was. He got to know everyone and would migrate from group to group, saying hello as he held his own Cup-of-Noodles or handful of cookies. He belonged! Even more amazing were the faces of my other students as they experienced the true joy of kindness and caring. These scenes would subsequently repeat themselves as more lost students found a home with us in that room. The most remarkable thing of all was that it all started because four seemingly tough guys cared enough to sound the alarm for a lonely kid they didn't even know. They had obviously been paying more attention in class than I thought.

Armando became a student of mine the next year as a sophomore. He fit well in a class full of other unique kids with special needs and caring mentors to help them. I learned that he was Autistic, giving me some frame of reference to his detached demeanor. He continued to be one of my students throughout high school, having me as his English teacher during his junior year and me having him as my TA, teacher's assistant, during his senior year. Our relationship continued to grow as he opened up to other students in class and felt comfortable in a safe environment where he was not only accepted, but also loved and appreciated.

Armando was a gifted artist and was always drawing in his notebook. While he was a TA for me during his senior year, he would love it when I asked him to use his skills to decorate the monthly calendar that I prominently displayed on the whiteboard in the back of my room. I used the calendar to reinforce the habit of planning with my students. I would initially list important school and class dates such as assemblies, final exam schedules, our Words of the Week, student birthdays, and speakers who would be coming to class. I had my students create their own calendars, include their own special dates when major tests and projects were due. They were required to keep this calendar in their binders and update it regularly.

A few days after posting the new calendar with these important dates, I would give Armando a list of weird and wacky holidays such as National Chocolate Chip Cookie Day, National Hug Your Pet Day, International Hat Day, and other silly celebrations. Armando would then adorn the calendar with the holidays that he chose which included his own artwork and clever sayings. When he finished with his creative contributions to our calendar, I would have my students take out their calendars and include days that they thought were interesting, fun, and important. They would stare at Armando's expert drawings and read his imaginative and funny quotes. They loved it! They would chatter and giggle about the different goofy holidays and Armando's creative additions. This always seemed to make Armando smile and puff out his chest with pride while watching these students appreciate his artistic ability and wit.

During Armando's senior year, he stopped coming to my class every day during Nutrition and Lunch. That worried me, so I asked some of the kids if they thought we did anything to hurt him or push him away. They told me not to worry. Armando had a new set of friends he hung around with during those times. I confirmed this with Armando who proudly told me that he had other friends, too, and they liked to hang out at different locations at school. He said that everything was okay because he was happy "out there" just like he was "in here". That really warmed my heart and reassured me that Armando was well on his way to confronting the world after he left our classroom cocoon.

When Armando graduated, my wife and I were honored to be included as guests at his family celebration of this important event. With grateful and wondrous tears in her eyes, Armando's mother shared her amazement and gratitude for the four boys who cared enough about him to intervene and point his life in a new direction. She told me how he was picked on constantly since the first grade and what a demoralizing impact that had on him. She also told me how his entire attitude about school and himself changed after our students had rescued, welcomed, accepted, and embraced him throughout high school. It was a beautiful day!

LEADERSHIP

"If you want to build a ship,
don't drum up the men to gather wood,
divide the work, and give orders.
Instead, teach them to yearn
for the vast and endless sea."

~ Antoine de Saint-Exupéry

SUPER SUPERINTENDENT SANDY

When I coached football, I used to say the same thing to my captains every year right after their teammates selected them to lead our teams. "Remember something. Your teammates picked you to be their captain because of who you are. Don't change. Don't think that you have to be someone or something different than who you are. They didn't vote for you to be their captain so you could boss them around, threaten them, and belittle their effort. They picked you because you make them feel important. Be an example. Lead with an open hand and not with a pointed finger or clenched fist. They will not follow you out of fear, but out of love and respect. That comes from your willingness to lead them as an equal, by being one of them. Don't ever forget that."

I say pretty much the same thing to our academic mentors as we train them for their new challenge. I tell them that they are their students' friends, but they are their mentors first. They are told to become and stay involved in the process, helping their students through assignments as well as personal issues that can derail any progress they have made. I implore them not to judge or chastise their students, reminding them that this will just alienate them. I emphasize strength, determination, patience, and consistency, telling them that their students will walk through the fires of Hell for them if they know that their mentors really care.

I have been fortunate to have had great leaders in my life, people who shaped me and countless others with their strength of character and commitment to do what is right. The best leader I have ever known is Sandy Thorstenson. She was an assistant principal at a school to which I applied as a teacher and head football coach many years ago. She was instrumental in me being selected for that job, and I worked very hard to make sure that she was not disappointed. She had a natural kindness about her and was genuine in every sense of the word. It was obvious where her priorities were. She cared about kids, all kids. She wanted them to be happy, self-confident, and successful. She also cared deeply about those who worked alongside her. Sandy was easy to approach and quick to give support whenever it was needed.

I was the latest in a long progression of coaches at that school who did not last very long. They no longer coached there because they were either apathetic or were excessively cruel and demoralizing to their athletes. There was not much excitement or enthusiasm in the hearts of the players when we began. There were not very many kids who even wanted to come out for football, so its teams were undermanned and overmatched by opponents. I was determined to change that.

Things started well. We recruited kids on campus to come out for spring football, telling them that we needed them and would be loyal to them in making their experience a positive one. A lot of boys participated in spring football that year, and we finished our practices with the biggest squad of varsity and junior varsity players that the school had in many years. Spring rolled into summer, and a large group of freshmen joined our program. Practices and weight training sessions were tough, but we coaches made sure that they were fun and positive, too.

Throughout this period of time, I made a concerted effort at inclusion and empathy. I met individually with players who were struggling with issues at home or with doubts about themselves as players. I talked and counseled and coached with every ounce of energy that I had. During this time, I was going through my own difficult circumstances. My parents were old and ill, so I took it upon myself to care for them, doing their shopping, preparing their meals, mowing their lawn, taking them to doctor appointments, and giving them constant assistance. I was trying to be the perfect son.

My wife was pregnant with our first son during this period, so I also made sure to make things as easy as possible for her. She had a demanding job, so I was diligent about doing work around the house and in the yard to help out as much as I could. I was trying to be the perfect husband and preparing to be the perfect parent. While this was all going on, I was also trying to be the perfect friend to guys who had gotten used to me being a sounding board for them as they faced their own problems. I was trying to be a perfect son, husband, friend, and now, I was trying to be the perfect coach for boys who had not had much compassionate guidance before I got there. When fall came, I also tried to be the perfect teacher, providing my students with great lessons and engaging enthusiasm. I didn't realize it at the time, but there was a storm brewing.

The season began well and the kids were happy. We were much better than teams had been in the past, but I put pressure on myself because we were not winning as much as I thought we needed to win to show our players that their hard work was paying off. The fact of the matter is that we were fine, but it was not enough for me. Knowing that there was so much negativity with past coaches,

I made sure to stay positive and encouraging, even when my spirits were at an all-time low. I just couldn't show it. I just couldn't let down my players, administrators, parents, wife, and friends. My solution was to just put more effort into everything I did. Then came a breaking point.

I had trouble sleeping during the summer, and it was getting worse in the fall. Initially, I would go to bed at a reasonable time but wake up three or four hours later with my mind racing about things I needed to do. I couldn't go back to sleep! It was like someone pushed the button on a blender in my head, and I couldn't turn it off. I would just get up and do some work, not wanting to waste the precious few hours I had. Soon, I began waking up after sleeping for two hours, and then after only an hour or so. I tried hard to get up without Gisele noticing. I didn't tell her because I didn't want to worry her, but I was getting very worried.

During the middle of that first season, I began waking up after sleeping for only thirty minutes or even less. I was constantly groggy, and it was extremely hard to concentrate. I became a shell of myself and was panicked about it. I had gone to the doctor to try to get some sleeping pills that would help me, but they didn't work. It was then that I became really desperate. I put on the best front I could with my classes, but got into the habit of closing the door to my classroom right after my students left and before the next class entered. I was so emotional and out of control! With my classroom door locked shut, I would walk to a back office that was attached to the room and just fall apart. I cried and I prayed as hard as I could. I kept asking God to help me find a way through this. I asked Him to get me through just one more class. Then, just before the bell rang to begin the next class, I would compose myself, wipe off my face, and greet my students with all the phony composure that I could muster. It was a horrible experience!

Finally, on the morning of one of our games, I fell apart. After not sleeping all night and trying to force sleep upon myself while lying there, I tried to get out of bed when the alarm clock rang. I took one step out of bed and hit the floor. I couldn't move. I couldn't think. I didn't know what to do. Gisele had become aware of my condition and was really worried. We talked about it. She insisted that I go directly to the doctor or even to the hospital to get some help. I insisted on going to school to prepare for our game. I won the argument but was in no condition to drive. She drove me to school and reminded me that she would be there after the game to pick me up. I never got that far.

One of my coaches was really worried about me and before school, he told Sandy what was going on. They both appeared in my classroom before any students arrived, and I just fell apart. I melted. I couldn't think or talk or even respond to her. She quickly called the office, arranged for a substitute, called Gisele, and told her that she would be taking me home. Before driving me home in what must have been a terribly shocking experience for her, Sandy called the district to arrange an appointment with a doctor. Gisele met us at home and then drove me directly to the doctor that Sandy had arranged.

I went to a hospital and was given some very strong medication that put me out for a long time. While I was experiencing the sleep that I had not known for months, Sandy and Gisele exchanged many calls as they arranged several appointments with doctors, a psychiatrist, and a psychologist. When I woke up, all I could think about was my team, my classes, Gisele, my parents, and all the trouble I had caused. Over time, I found out that I was suffering from depression that had not been addressed when it should have been. It was months before I talked to anyone other than Gisele. She took care of me but must have been petrified. She was within weeks of giving birth to our first child, and her husband was a complete wreck.

I was ashamed and embarrassed about what had happened. Back then, depression or having a "nervous breakdown" had a powerfully negative stigma. It was especially hard for me to face because I had always been the strong one, the person others came to for help. Being helpless myself was more than I could accept. I felt that I let everyone down. Even though Sandy and others at my school urged me to return, I was too ashamed to do that, so after months at home,

I accepted a job managing a sports photography business, a position I once had before returning to coaching.

I did well in my new job, one without the expectations of being all things to all people. The company grew and I was given raises and promotions during my two years there. During this time, Sandy kept in touch with me. She was such a compassionate, encouraging soul! We'd have lunch or talk on the phone, and she would remind me of the positive things that happened while I coached and taught at her school. We discussed my eventual return to education, but I fought hard against the idea even though I knew that I was meant to teach.

Less than two years after I met her, Sandy was named as the new principal at my old high school, the place where I played and coached for many years. She asked me to come back. My old coach would be the head coach and all I had to do was to teach and be his assistant. Gisele and I talked long and hard about this and knew that, as frightening as it was, it was the right decision, so I returned to education. I never left again. I had learned my own limitations and inability to be the "perfect" anything. All I needed to do was to be my best. It is a lesson and opportunity that changed my life. I taught and coached there for several years before making another big change.

Sandy eventually accepted the position as superintendent of our school district, and I left my old school to become the head coach at La Serna. Sandy and I remained close friends, and she would always stop by to talk when she visited our school. She was a strong leader who led with conviction and compassion. I would always marvel at her natural goodness and humility. Even though she experienced tremendous success as superintendent and received state and even national acclaim, she was never too busy to stop and talk to students and teachers, making every one of them feel important and cared for. I would watch her pick up pieces of trash and throw them away as she walked through the school. She was enormously powerful yet never above doing something like that. Everyone who has ever known her loves and respects her. She is an amazingly extraordinary human being and the best leader I have ever seen.

In the same year that I was selected as a California State Teacher of the Year, she was selected as the California State Superintendent of the Year. The irony was not lost on me. I would have never returned to teaching had it not been for her. She could have easily done the easy thing and moved on from the disaster of my meltdown. Instead, she saw something in me, gave me an opportunity, and nurtured me as a teacher more than anyone will ever know. She is a great leader because of many things, but mostly because of her heart. On the night I spoke at the ceremony in Sacramento for my Teacher of the Year award, the first thing I did was introduce my personal guardian angel, Sandy Thorstenson, who had been honored earlier that day on the floor of the California State Senate for her leadership and incredible achievements as a superintendent. It was a special moment, one that I hold deep in my own heart.

28

KINDNESS

*"Kind words can be short and easy to speak,
but their echoes are truly endless."*

~ Mother Teresa

NATHANIEL

Nathaniel was a truly unique and special young man who was wise beyond his years. He was an academic mentor in our program and took his job very seriously. While I missed several weeks of school due to back surgery during Nathaniel's senior year, he assumed the responsibility of maintaining our practice of having short, meaningful activities every Tuesday. We called them "AcTuesities" so that, in my frenetic constant sprint through each day, I would not forget to include them every week. When I returned to work, I heard from both my substitute and students about what a remarkable job Nathaniel did in my absence, leading "AcTuesities" in other classes as well as in his own.

Hearing this, I asked Nathaniel to step outside my classroom and told him how grateful and proud of him that I was. He described many of the activities that he created on his own or learned about while doing research on the internet. One of these activities was so powerful that I made sure to include it with every class that followed.

In that activity, Nathaniel gave everyone a blank piece of paper. Then, standing in front of the class, he told everyone to crumble up their piece of paper into a little ball. Then, he asked them to open up the paper ball and try to straighten the pieces of paper out, removing all the wrinkles while saying, "I'm sorry" over and over again. He described the obvious to the class of bewildered students. No matter how hard anyone tries, once the paper is wrinkled, it can never return to its previous smooth state. Then he told them that the papers were like other people and the wrinkles represented our words to them. He said that when we say something hurtful to others, we make wrinkles that will always be there even if we try hard to remove them and apologize many times. He said that positive comments make wrinkles, too, and we should always be careful not to make wrinkles that will forever cause pain and to make sure that the wrinkles we leave make others better and stronger.

That was an awesome lesson, describing the lasting impression that our words have on others. I thanked Nathaniel for the lesson and for his amazing leadership while I was recovering from surgery. After graduation from high school, he became a United States Marine. I was grateful that someone as special as Nathaniel would be protecting all of us.

29

TRANSFORMATION

"Scared and sacred
are spelled with the same letters.
Awful proceeds from
the same root word as awesome.
Terrify and terrific.
Every negative experience
holds the seed of transformation."

~ Alan Cohen

NEIL

While working with my at-risk students, I have had to learn a brutal truth. Despite our best efforts and all the guidance we try to give, there are students who don't recognize the opportunity in front of them and don't make it. In my first few years in the program, this was the hardest lesson for me to learn. I want to save all my students, and when they disregard the lessons we try to teach and continue on their personal spirals downward, it is painful to accept. It used to eat at me to the point that I couldn't sleep and became overly emotional when we would lose one of these kids. Experience and a lot of heartache taught me that if I crumbled every time a kid was pulled downward more powerfully than we tried to pull upward, I would soon be of no use to the many kids who were making strides in the right direction. I had to establish a balance between caring and practicality if I were to continue helping the teenagers constantly sent to me. It's taken a while, and I sometimes still dip my toe into the waters of unrealistic expectations; but I have developed an awareness that we just can't save them all.

Neil seemed to be one of the youngsters that we just couldn't save. He came to me as a sophomore with tremendous ability as a football player who had flunked out of his previous school. Attracted by La Serna's strong football program and OASIS, Neil's parents transferred him to La Serna, giving me the challenge of turning this boy around. He looked like a good football player with his stout muscular frame that stretched over six feet in height. He had long blond hair that framed an overly confident face. I learned about him from our football coaches who told me that, if we could turn him around, Neil would be a big asset to the varsity football team. I was encouraged by his identity as a football player, hoping to capitalize on my experience as a coach. We quickly established a good relationship, talking about football and his goals to become the best linebacker in the area. I felt that we had a good foundation on which to build. Then came our parent meeting.

Knowing how important parent involvement is in changing attitudes and behavior in teenagers, I have a mandatory parent meeting every year in the early fall with the students, parents, mentors, and me to explain our program and its expectations.

"Mandatory" has sadly become a bad word in today's public schools. Laws intended to maintain equity for students have led to school and district edicts to "rethink and rephrase" this word, avoiding it at all costs. I understand the inherent problems with mandatory requirements, but I use it, without apology, in eliciting parent involvement in their at-risk students' journey to become successful.

I give a few options for evenings on which to attend. I tell everyone that, if parents or guardians don't show up and meet on one of these evenings, I will call them continually until we are able to meet during the school day when I can introduce the mentor to the parent and describe the process that we have to undertake together. If, even after these repeated calls, we can't get the parent or guardian to come to school, I make a home visit to speak to students and parents there. Because I have a history of following through with what I tell them I will do, we usually end up with almost 100 percent participation.

It was at this parent meeting in the fall of Neil's sophomore year that I learned the extent of his problems. After a general introduction of our program to everyone in attendance, I have students, parents, and mentors meet together in small groups to discuss the things that mentors will do every day to help their assigned students. It was during this portion of the meeting when I was approached by a lady wearing sunglasses.

"Hi. I'm Neil's mom. He and his dad couldn't come tonight because...." Her voice trailed off and became soft, and I could see that she was crying. Neil had been found passed out and lying on the grass in front of McDonalds that afternoon. Neil had overdosed on some pills and had to be taken to the hospital where his stomach was pumped. The mother's tears turned into sobs as she described the ongoing war that she and her husband were waging against the drugs that Neil refused to stop taking.

Hearing that information was like being doused with a bucket of cold water. Drugs are the most insidious and formidable enemy of salvation for lost children. They lure kids into continued use with sweet release from their problems and then grip their necks in a death hold that is often too difficult to break. I learned from Neil's mother that his use of drugs had been a growing problem for quite a while, and this news froze me with dread.

A few days after the meeting, Neil returned to school. I had a talk with him outside the classroom and quickly learned he didn't share his parents' and my fear of his continued drug use. His cavalier "it's no big deal" attitude stood clearly in stark contrast to the reality of his situation.

"Neil, you could have died the other night! Do you realize that?"

He didn't flinch as he told me that he had it all under control. He would just be more careful next time. My extended explanation of what this would lead to and my insistence that the only real intelligent choice was to stop using all drugs was met with almost no reaction. It was obvious that Neil had no intention of ending his involvement with drugs. I have to be honest. My hope for his success in turning his life around became very dim at that point. I told him that I would continue to try to convince him that he was wrong in ignoring the real dangers of drugs, but deep in my heart, I was preparing myself for what I thought was the inevitability of his downfall.

I called his parents and his school guidance counselor, sharing what I knew as well as my deep concern. I pledged my commitment to work with him to remove this danger from his life. I warn all of my students that I will "lovingly harass them" in my efforts to change destructive habits and behaviors, and I always make good on my promises. I spoke to Neil often about a myriad of things, ranging from his disrespect of others (including teachers) to his refusal to complete his schoolwork and his use of drugs. "Hey, man, if I didn't care about you, I wouldn't bug you all the time. It's a pain in my butt, too, but it's a pain I'll gladly accept if it means saving your life." He'd roll his eyes and then smile, trying to charm me to get me off his back.

Watching teenagers continue making bad and often dangerous choices is like being in a helicopter and watching them run blindly, like lemmings, toward a treacherous cliff with a long drop to the jagged rocks below. I can see them and where they're going, screaming at them, begging them to stop, but their mindless instinct to just follow the lemmings in front of them is sometimes too strong to halt their fatal sprint. Despite their total disregard for my screaming warnings, I continue to yell, plead, and beg them to stop. I need shepherds on the ground to turn them in a different direction, and my shepherds are the students' mentors. Tracy was Neil's shepherd, and she worked hard to reroute his sprint toward disaster.

We made progress, but it was sporadic and stressful. Neil would seem to get better and then suddenly change direction and run toward the cliff. Countless conversations in and outside the classroom yielded little lasting results, so it was no shock when we learned, one day, that Neil had been discovered high as a kite during one of his classes. Because of our school's zero tolerance drug policy, he was suspended and then expelled for his choice to use drugs at school. He was sent to another local high school in an effort to remove him from his social circle at La Serna and give him a new start. When that happened, I thought that I would never see Neil again.

More than a year later, I was in my classroom in late August, preparing for the start of a new school year. As I was working there alone, the door opened, and Neil walked in. He told me that he finally got his act together and was given a chance to complete his senior year at La Serna. He informed me that he would also be playing football, but as a defensive lineman and not as the linebacker he had always wanted to be. During his absence, La Serna had developed other linebackers, returning starters, who had cemented their positions with their outstanding performances the previous year.

"It's okay, Mr. LaVigne. I just wanna play. I actually like being a defensive lineman. I just wanted to come by and see you. I want you to know that I remember all the things you tried to teach me, and, well, it finally sunk in. I didn't like where I was or who I was. I got tired of seeing my parents disappointed. I want to make them proud. I want to make you proud."

"Neil, just seeing you here and hearing you say that makes me proud. I want you to WIN. What does that mean?"

Reciting the words of an acronym that I taught him almost two years earlier, he said, "What's Important Now."

"And what does NOW mean?"

He smiled as he said, "No Opportunity Wasted."

"Okay. That's good. You remembered. Just don't forget. This is a one-time opportunity. Don't screw it up!"

He followed with a question, "You gonna come watch me play?"

"I wouldn't miss it for the world! Now get your butt out to the practice field and be the hardest working guy out there. Got it?"

"I got it, Coach," he assured me and gave me a hug before leaving.

Neil was still no angel in school that fall, but he managed to stay out of big trouble. He became a starter on the varsity team, performing well and making big plays to lead his team to a championship season. I went to every game, watched him play, and after he greeted and hugged his parents during post-game rituals, he would always stop in the midst of his celebrating teammates and find me on the field. As soon as he spotted me, he'd run over and give me my own big hug.

"How'd I do?" he'd ask.

"You did great! I'm proud of you, Neil. I love you."

The coolest part of our post-game exchange was when he'd say, without hesitation or embarrassment, "I love you, too, Mr. LaVigne." That made me feel like a king, and I'd finish with, "Now go celebrate with your buddies." He'd then stride off, slapping teammates and coaches on the shoulder as he made his way to the waiting bus. I'd watch him all the way until he disappeared into the bus.

A few years after he graduated, he stopped by my classroom after school one day. This time, he brought his wife and little son to show me. He told me that he had a job in construction, and was going to be a good husband and father. This time, I didn't doubt him one bit.

30

PLAYFULNESS

"Playfulness, dear friends, is what manifests love.
Love is not manifested through
serious survivability, seriousness, stability.
Love, the essence of love,
manifests itself through playfulness."

~ Réné Gaudette

NICK

Nick came to me as a sophomore after failing all but one of his classes during his freshman year. Ryan, his mentor, was a very serious young man whose patience would be repeatedly tested by this tall Armenian kid who had the disposition of a cuddly puppy. That puppy was also too playful and frustratingly lazy. Day after day, I'd watch Ryan pester and cajole Nick during class, employing every tactic imaginable to make his mentee more serious and responsible. He was usually successful, but there were times that Nick would squirrel around so much that he would anger his normally stoic mentor, leading to louder, harsher words of admonishment. Nick would do things just to get under Ryan's skin, watching for a reaction like a young child excitedly waits for a Christmas gift. He'd watch and wait for Ryan's patience to run out, and then when his mentor's frustration was at a boiling point, Nick would hug him and say, "I love you, Ryan!" as Ryan squirmed to free himself from the embrace of his goofy student.

Ryan's persistence and patience paid off. As a sophomore, Nick passed all but one of his classes. This was a tremendous improvement, but lacking credits that he should have earned as a freshman, Nick had to attend both summer school and adult school classes to catch up. He'd vacillate between determination and distracted lack of effort, but he managed to pass all of his classes as a junior, earning a grade point average that would place him in the top third of his graduating class. He continued his playful, silly routine in my junior English class. Out of nowhere, he'd walk over to me and say, "You look like you need a big hug, Mr. LaVigne. Come here. Give old Nick a big hug."

"Get away from me, you weirdo. Get back to work," I'd say.

"Rejection is a tough thing to overcome, Mr. LaVigne. I hope I'm not scarred for life."

"Doggone it, Nick! Quit screwin' around!"

He got the reaction he wanted from me and would slowly return to his seat after stopping by a few classmates, asking, "And how's your day going? Do you need a hug?" flashing his puppy dog eyes. His classmates always got a kick out of him, and so did I, but his antics made conducting a productive class nearly impossible.

During his junior year, Nick was helped by Justin, another outstanding mentor with a calm demeanor and a huge heart. Justin had the patience of Job, working hard to assist Nick and his other mentees despite their periodic lapses of resolve and judgment. His students gathered around him at a table in the back of the room, and he was like a finely crafted clock, ticking away evenly, steadily through their frowns and frequent resistance. Nick was his biggest challenge because he had such great natural intelligence that was often dominated by his even bigger natural tendency to be excessively playful. When Nick would drift into his "Do you need a hug?" routine, Justin would just look up and shake his head without relinquishing control. He definitely reined Nick in more tightly which was made possible by his strength of leadership, Nick's maturity from being a year older, and the foundation that Ryan laid the year before.

Nick's grades improved and his credits lost as a freshman were recovered by the end of his junior year, so he decided to go out for the basketball team. He made the varsity squad, and despite receiving limited playing time, he was proud of this achievement. He was also immensely proud of the fact that he was graduating from high school. He had taken us all on a playful, fun, spontaneous, and sometimes nail-biting journey, but he graduated with a 3.0 grade point average.

He surprised me with a few serious words on the evening of his graduation. "Mr. LaVigne, my family is really proud of me, and I want you to know that I would never have made it without you. I'm serious this time. I need a hug." He hugged me straight-faced and sincere. I had waited a long time for that hug, and yes, I needed it, too. Then, he took his place next to me as we took our annual group photo of our graduating seniors. There he is, forever, smiling that mischievous yet engaging smile that drove us all crazy but made every day an adventure.

31

PERSISTENCE

*"Dripping water hollows out stone,
not through force but through persistence."*

~ Ovid

ERYN AND REGINA

'm not the most religious or righteous person in the world, but I have tremendous faith in God. I am a Christian. I'm not one to preach or give the appropriate Scriptural reference because I'm just not qualified. I simply have a deep and strong faith in God and His plan for us all. I have often said that the most Christian person I have ever known was a Buddhist. His name is Ron Imada.

Ron was a high school friend, classmate, and teammate of mine on our football team. He was the quarterback and I was the center, giving us plenty of potential for silly remarks about me snapping the ball to him on our quarterback-center exchange. We continued our experience as teammates when we both played football at Rio Hondo College. He switched to defense, playing free safety while I remained at center, but our friendship grew and he remains one of my closest friends to this day.

I believe that God cares a lot more about the sincerity of our heart than He does about the name of our church. Ron embodies all the qualities that I feel Christians should have. He is incredibly humble, sincere, unselfish, caring, and empathetic. His first concern is always the welfare of others. He, his wife Sharon, and children Brett and Eryn are like family to us. We are very, very close to them all. That is why it was such a blessing for me to have both Eryn and Brett as students in high school. Once again, I lucked out by having close friends live in the attendance area of La Serna High School where I teach.

Brett was a student in my English class and Eryn was an academic mentor during our first year of our OASIS program for at-risk students. Both Brett and Eryn are great reflections of their wonderful, caring parents.

Eryn began her experience as an academic mentor as all my students do, being assigned two students whose academic and social backgrounds are dramatically different than her own. Regina was one of those students. She did not come from a troubled home infested with drugs, violence, and turmoil. She was simply a girl who was lost. She had no other school goals than to totally immerse herself in the social atmosphere of high school. She was much more concerned about her clothes, makeup, friends, and boys than she was concerned about her schoolwork. The inevitable conflicts and drama of teenage life consumed her as did her complete focus on her appearance, popularity, and social status. It was easy to see that getting her on the right path toward academic success would be a unique and challenging task.

Eryn was a quiet, friendly, and reserved student whose outward demeanor belied her strong sense of not only commitment to her academic excellence, but of her natural instinct to have fun. She was a tall, beautiful, and popular girl whose smile reflected her inner beauty and ability to see others as equal partners in experiencing the joy of everyday life. For many reasons, Eryn was a total pleasure to have in class every day.

When Eryn began her service as a mentor, I had no idea that she would become such a strong, mature, and persistent influence on her students. At the beginning of class, she would smile and engage her students in trivial banter that is normal in teenagers, but it didn't take long before she became an exacting taskmaster, scowling at her students when they got off-task while she slid assignments in front of them to do. It was very enjoyable to see this quiet, kind soul shift into her drill sergeant persona and become such a strong soldier of change. Eryn was exceptional in getting the most out of her students.

Predictably, Regina resisted Eryn's constant insistence to get work done, rolling her eyes and shaking her head at her new role model. That didn't faze Eryn in the least. She was persistent in demanding responsibility and effort from Regina. Within weeks, the results were evident. Eryn connected with Regina by listening to her dramatic accounts of this girl or that boy who said or did something to upset her. Like clockwork, Eryn would transition from this empathetic confidante to a focused mentor who made sure that Regina completed her assignments and realized the importance of investing time at home to do her homework. Regina's grades, behavior, and attitude improved dramatically. She also seemed happier and more self-assured. It was an amazing thing to see.

After the end of Regina's first year in our program with Eryn as her guide, she continued to improve her grades, attendance, and behavior, completing the year with a 2.67 grade point average after failing almost all of her classes as a freshman. Her trajectory was set and she finished her junior year with a 3.17 grade point average. She kept in contact with her first-year mentor, Eryn, who continued her strong influence and encouragement while she was away at college. Regina applied to be an academic mentor herself during her senior year and did an extraordinary job as the first OASIS student to become a mentor, helping one of her own at-risk students to raise his initial grade point average from 0.83 to 3.50. She also participated in student government, serving on the ASB cabinet. Regina completed her first semester as a senior with a 3.83 grade point average, and it was time to give her the recognition she deserved.

During the spring of Regina's senior year, I was asked by our assistant principal to nominate a student who had overcome obstacles and made significant improvement in academic achievement for an award given by the Association of California School Administrators. I knew immediately that I was going to nominate Regina. I submitted my nomination, explaining the nuances in her climb to great grades and an equally impressive growth in becoming a leader on campus.

In the spring of Regina's senior year, we were informed that she had been selected as one of only seventeen students from the entire state to win this award. She, her parents, our school administrators, my wife, and I joined hundreds of others at an elaborate event that celebrated this achievement. It was a formal dinner ceremony and it was awesome to see the pride in Regina's eyes as well as in the eyes of her parents when her story was told and she walked to the front of the crowded room. She stood there in her moment of glory, and all I could think about was the persistent dedication of Eryn, Regina's dutiful mentor, who helped shape her life. Eryn was away at college and unable to attend the event, but I was proud and overjoyed enough for both of us.

Regina continued her academic excellence throughout high school, graduated, and went on to college. Years after her high school graduation, a group of my friends gathered at the home of Ron and Sharon Imada, Eryn's parents, before we left for our annual Christmas dinner, a tradition that we continue over forty years after we graduated high school ourselves. I noticed a beautiful blue dress hanging in the hallway while we waited for our other friends to arrive and joked with my friends, "Hey. Are you guys going to some fancy party or something? Look at this dress! Holy moly! You're going to knock 'em dead, Sharon."

"That's not my mine. That's Eryn's dress! She's going to a concert with Regina next week."

I was blown away by the fact that this mentor and student still had such a strong connection. I realized that Eryn's persistence in leading her initially reluctant student had not only resulted in better grades and a better life, but was the force that created a lifelong appreciation and friendship.

32

FOCUS

"Focusing is about saying no."

~ Steve Jobs

MITCHELL

Mitchell was one of those kids who was totally enamored with technology and the internet. Evidence of this was his habit of falling asleep during class due to his patrolling of the web into the wee hours of the night, often extending to two or three o'clock in the morning. He was a bright, pleasant boy with a natural goodness about him, but he was one of the most distracted students I have ever seen. His sandy blond hair flopped down on his childlike face, and he always seemed disconnected from any and all classroom tasks. He had the attention span of a hummingbird when he was awake during class, getting up from his seat every five to ten minutes to grab a dictionary he didn't need to use or cruising the classroom, chatting with other students in prolonged periods of absence from where he belonged. He was taking medication for Attention Deficit Disorder, but it didn't seem to be doing him a lot of good.

"Mitchell, what are you doing? Get back to your seat and get to work." I must have said that to him a thousand times. He'd smile and return to his table, but within just a few minutes, he was up and about again. It was exhausting, and I spoke to his mother and counselor many times about his problem, pleading for a change in medication and stricter rules about his use of the computer and internet at home. It was a struggle that continued through his junior year. He passed most of his classes and attended adult school to make up the credits he needed for graduation, but he remained far behind in accumulating essential credits. It was a serious and constant concern.

Midway through his senior year, it became apparent that, if something miraculous didn't happen, Mitchell would not be graduating with his classmates, so I asked for a meeting with his counselor, the assistant principal, Mitchell's mother, and all of his teachers. At the meeting, I expressed my fear that he wasn't going to make it. I asked for us all to come up with a final battle plan that would give him a chance to cross the finish line and graduate. During the meeting, we looked at his transcript and current class schedule. It became obvious that Mitchell was going to have to do more than any student I have ever seen do in a startlingly short amount of time. In the second semester, he would have to add a class, giving him seven classes instead of the typical six that other students had. He would also have to take three adult school classes and a Saturday class that lasted four hours every week. The biggest hurdle was the fact that he had to pass all of these classes to graduate.

When we laid these facts on the table, I looked at Mitchell and saw a look of terror in his tear-filled eyes. He didn't say a word, but he looked frightened and fragile, hearing things that overwhelmed him. It was as though a huge wave of reality was coming down on him, and he was frozen with fear. I reached out and grabbed his arm, telling him, "Mitchell, this isn't going to be easy, but you can do it. What you have to remember is that everyone in this room wants you to make it, and we're going to be right next to you as you take each step." He looked me dead in the face, and his eyes became pools filled with tears that ran down his face as he sat motionless.

I made the commitment to call his home every night to make sure that he had attended adult school that day and was working on his homework instead of playing on the computer. I asked his mother to make sure that he never stayed up later than 11:00 PM during the week and spent at least half of his weekend on schoolwork. There wasn't much confidence in that room as we ended the meeting, but we all agreed to do whatever it took to help Mitchell. Before parting ways, I grabbed his shoulders and reminded him that he wasn't alone in this process. We would all be there to help him. That finally led him to give me a little smile. "I'll try," he said.

I sounded like Yoda from Star Wars as I told him, "There is no try, Mitchell. You WILL do it!"

That second semester was a flurry of classes and calls home to check on his progress. His back was against the wall, but he responded like a champion! He attended and passed all of his classes, finally graduating from La Serna to the amazement and delight of all of us. This monumental effort and his success in climbing this mountain of work changed Mitchell in a way that none of us could have predicted. He graduated with a confidence in himself that he had never experienced before. The next year, he attended community college while having a full-time job. When he visited on several occasions, he was clearly not the distracted, lost kid I knew for most of his high school years. He had goals, a plan to achieve them, and a tenacity that would make any parent or teacher proud. It was a long road with a treacherous final ascent, but he finished his journey with focus, confidence, and self-respect, emerging as a man and not a frightened boy.

33

LOYALTY

*"The scholar does not consider gold and jade to be
precious treasures, but loyalty and good faith."*

~ Confucius

JIMMY

When I was an assistant coach at my old high school, I came to know players with whom I strongly identified. They were scrappier and more determined than they were athletically skilled. Football was an escape for them, an escape from problems that are typical in teenage boys. Football was extremely important to them, and they worked relentlessly to achieve their dreams of individual and team success. I became especially close to one of these young men.

Gisele and I gave our second son Mark the middle name James after one of my linemen, James "Jimmy" Hope. He was an amazing young man on many levels. He was our center and the anchor of our offensive line. He was not tall, all of 5'9" but weighed about

250 pounds. He was rock-solid and one of the fiercest competitors I have ever coached. He was strong as an ox and very intelligent. He wasn't, however, the prototypical physical specimen to play such an integral role on our team, so during the off-season before Jimmy's junior year, Coach Mahlstede approached me with what he felt was a major concern.

"LaVigne, we gotta find a center!" he insisted.

"What are you talking about?" I replied. "We have a starting center, and he's gonna be the best you've ever had. Jimmy Hope's our starting center."

"Bullshit, LaVigne! Hope's too slow and squatty. He's never gonna block the nose men and linebackers he's gonna face!"

"Sure he will! He's the strongest, toughest kid we have and he's also the hardest working guy in the weight room. He's a leader! Don't worry about center. Trust me. I know what I'm doing."

It's a good thing he did trust me because Jimmy Hope went on to be first team All-CIF for two straight years, something no other player had ever accomplished at Santa Fe before. He was great in every aspect of his game, making and adjusting blocking calls on the line of scrimmage and destroying anyone who lined up against him. He also had a mean streak and was fiercely loyal to me as well as to his team. He once did something during a game that still makes me laugh every time I think about it.

During games, my offensive line would report to me on the sideline right after they got off the field. I would have my dry erase board there and would calmly review the fronts they had just seen, making adjustments on the board that we would implement in our next offensive series. Coach Mahlstede was very emotional on the sidelines and would periodically display his intensity like a lightning bolt, striking with stunning ferocity. A few times each season, he would stomp toward our group on the sideline during one of our sessions, charging like some frenzied bear toward another animal. He would grab the dry erase board away from me and throw it to the ground as he yelled, challenging us to just go out and physically destroy our opponent.

"This isn't a drafting class! This is football! All you need to know is that you gotta go out and kick the crap out of the guy in front of you. It's no secret! It's no mystery! Just go out there and kick someone's ass!"

To be honest, Coach Mahlstede had great instincts and could tell when there was a dip in the team's sense of urgency. I have come to realize that his actions on the sideline, just like those on the practice field, were as calculated as they were spontaneous. He certainly got everyone's attention, and his success in producing championship teams is evidence that he always knew exactly what he was doing.

My job, however, was to make sure that my players knew WHO we should block and beat into submission. I was used to Coach's eruptions and knew that it was just a manifestation of the passion of our head coach during the heat of battle. I accepted it but never knew when it was coming. During a very close and heated game during Jimmy's senior season, Coach Mahlstede approached on his charge. I would typically rest the dry erase board on my knee with my foot on the bench as my players watched. This time, Jimmy was standing at the other end of the board. As Coach went to grab the board and hurl it to the turf, Jimmy grabbed hold and wouldn't let go. In a comical scene that lasted about thirty seconds, Coach yanked on the board, unable to pull it away from a very intense center who had no time for this. They wrestled back and forth for control of the board until Coach Mahlstede finally gave up and stomped away, yelling, "To Hell with this! Just do your job!"

All my linemen giggled as we finished our sideline meeting. Jimmy just stared at me with a big grin and gave me a victorious wink. We laughed our heads off as the players shoved their helmets on and sprinted back on the field for our next offensive series of plays.

We ended up destroying our opponent that night, scoring over forty points against a very strong defense. I spent much of the night after that game convincing Coach Mahlstede that Jimmy's actions and the other players' reaction had nothing to do with disrespect or defiance. I told him that they loved and respected him immensely but were simply focused on making the adjustments that we needed to win the game. Jimmy was loyal to him, but he was also loyal to me and to his group. He meant no harm. Coach Mahlstede bought it, and I was relieved.

After all these years, Jimmy and I still laugh our heads off about that incident. Our coach-player relationship has grown into a deep and strong friendship. In the final years of my coaching career, he was often a fixture on the sidelines during our games. When I faced a longtime nemesis who coached against me from across the field, Jimmy would stand right next to me or even in front of me on the sideline, staring down my opponent. He was fiercely loyal, and his presence reassured me and made me grateful to have crossed paths with this special human being. He went on to become a published poet and English teacher at a local high school. His students are lucky because he undoubtedly conducts his classes with the same fiery intensity and enthusiasm that he had as a football player. I am also loyal to him, and there is nothing I wouldn't do to help him if he needed it. He remains one of my most beloved and respected players and friends.

34

ACCOUNTABILITY

"You reap what you sow."

~ Galatians 6:7

ALEX

When I introduce the core values to my students at the beginning of the school year, I always start with accountability. It is the cornerstone of everything we do. I believe that for the most part, we all create our personal destinies by first accepting responsibility for everything we say and do, realizing that these words and actions affect others in a very powerful way. The best example of this is the story about Alex, a young man I coached many years ago.

My first real job as a football coach occurred when I was in my early twenties at my old high school. Jack Mahlstede, my former head coach and life's greatest mentor, gave me this opportunity, starting my own coaching journey. I was assigned to coach the varsity offensive and defensive linemen. I was excited as I began to work with my players, wanting to do the best for them and expecting the best from them. I was, however, given a warning and directive from Coach Mahlstede regarding one of my players. His name was Alex.

Alex was a defensive lineman who was fairly big and incredibly quick. His natural physical ability was completely aligned with what I knew we needed at his position. He was quick, tough, and explosive. He was also a gang member who had a reputation for doing things his way. He was also exceedingly quiet, giving him an unmistakable mystique that elicited fear and respect in his teammates. Stories of his violent behavior preceded him, adding to his teammates' fear of him. Before practice even began, Coach Mahlstede told me that I could not treat Alex like the other players. He didn't like and would not accept discipline. I had to just try to teach him what I could and let him play. Coach told me that Alex would not respond if I tried to make him change.

I realized it then and even more now that Coach's instructions came more from his desire to "save" Alex as they did from his desire to win games. He had come to know Alex well and realized that football was a big part of his salvation. Coach didn't want to risk losing him to the streets by having him quit. He was trying to turn this kid's life around and strongly felt that Alex would walk away from football if we pushed him too hard. It's just another example of my former coach's big heart.

Alex was a true gang member. There were many stories about him kicking the crap out of other guys in fights and not hesitating to use more than his fists to exact pain and his personal justice on others. I have never seen a player who was feared more by his teammates than Alex.

Wanting to please my old coach and current boss, I tried to do what he said even though it went against my instinct to treat all players the same. I was careful not to speak loudly when I corrected Alex's technique so that I did not embarrass him. I tolerated his lack of effort in drills, knowing that when he lined up to play in real game situations, he would deliver. I did what I was instructed to do during the initial weeks of the season, but when we had our scrimmage against perennial power Loyola, I just could not accept his behavior and I reacted.

During the scrimmage, we had just finished our first offensive series when we switched to defense. I clapped loudly, telling our defense to get on the field. Everybody ran to the huddle except for Alex. He just casually strolled onto the field and took his place in the huddle. He played with ferocity but was often misaligned and missed some of his basic reads. I tried hard to restrain myself, walking up to Alex to correct him when he made mistakes. His reaction to each of my attempts to coach him, however, was to stare at me defiantly and to continue to make the same mistakes over and over. He also played dirty, taking cheap shots at players after the whistle blew. I became increasingly frustrated but kept my cool. Soon, our defense was called off the field as the offense sprinted to its huddle. Alex took off his helmet and walked off the field as his teammates ran to the sidelines. I was running out of patience.

He repeated his lack of discipline and hustle during the second series of plays, and I was losing my mind. When the defense was called onto the field for the third time, Alex seemed to walk more slowly than before to the huddle and gave me that "Don't mess with me" stare as I took my place next to the huddle. He did not even make it to the huddle in time to get the defensive call. He was more concerned with trying to intimidate and challenge me. He picked the wrong guy.

"Okay, Alex, you're out! Give me a new nose man!" He scowled at me and didn't even move as a few players sprinted onto the field to take his place. I walked over to him and quietly told him to "Get your ass off the field or you're gonna be really embarrassed." He shook his head and smirked as he slowly used his gangster strut in moving to the sideline.

Right away, I could see Coach Mahlstede's reaction to what I did. He was not happy. He walked over to me and growled, "I thought I told you not to single him out like that!"

"Coach, I'm sorry, but I can't be somebody I'm not. I don't care how good he is. He's part of this team and I'll hold him accountable just like all the other guys. If you can't accept that, you're gonna have to fire me."

Coach Mahlstede mumbled and shook his head as he walked away from me. I saw him seething on the sidelines as we completed the scrimmage without Alex playing another down. After addressing the team following the scrimmage, Coach approached me with a "What the Hell are you doing?" line of questioning. I listened respectfully but repeated what I had previously told him.

"Coach, I don't care how good the guy is. If he is lazy, defiant, and undisciplined, he's gonna hurt us on the field. His attitude is also a cancer. If we let him act like that, it's gonna affect the entire team. We can't win with negative attitudes and without discipline. Hell! YOU taught me that!"

My old coach found it difficult to argue against that, so he once again shook his head in disgust and walked away. I spotted Alex and walked up to him. He looked at me with hatred in his eyes, but I still told him what he needed to hear, "Alex, you're a tough guy and you can be a great football player but not if you don't do the things we need you to do. I'm sorry, man. If you want to play and be a part of this thing, you are going to have to do what I say. I'm looking for hustle, discipline, and desire. Show me that, and you're on the field. If you don't, you might as well quit because I can't and won't baby you." He just stared at me as I walked away.

I think my final words about not being willing to baby him got his attention. He obviously didn't like the idea of him being a baby, and although he still gave me icy stares, he began to change. As the days and weeks went by, he started to listen to me when I coached him and he ran on and off the field just like his teammates. I played him because he did what I asked, and he became a real force on our defense, the player that opposing offenses feared most. Then came his biggest lesson of all.

Our linemen met in the team room on game days at 4:30 PM sharp. I expected my players to get dressed and taped right after our team meal so that they would be on time for this meeting where we would finalize and review everything we would be doing in the game. I had a rule. If a player was late to the meeting and he was a starter, he lost his starting position and I would substitute another player for him. If a player was second string and not a starter, he might as well plan on not being in the game. There were no excuses and no exceptions.

It was midseason and we were preparing to play Dominguez, an excellent team that would be our biggest obstacle for a league championship. I waited anxiously in the team room before the meeting, knowing that everyone was there, everyone except Alex. When the second hand on the clock hit twelve at 4:30, I closed the door and locked it. I told the players not to open it no matter what happened. I also told Jaime, a skinny but tough and quick kid, he would be starting as nose man that night. Jaime was excited and started to hyperventilate, but I could see the fear grow in his eyes as he realized that he would be replacing Alex, the last guy on Earth that anyone wanted to anger.

About five minutes into our meeting, there was a knock on the door. Players looked at each other, wondering what would happen next. I told them not to open the door and calmly continued the meeting. Knocks turned into loud banging and Alex's voice threatening, "Open the fucking door!" I acted like nothing was happening and continued the meeting until we were finished.

When the meeting was done, I told the players that they had fifteen minutes to get their gear and meet in the weight room before we board the bus. I opened the door to let them out and saw Alex sitting on the steps that led down to our team room. The players filed out of the room, moving quickly and making sure not to have eye contact with Alex. After they all made their way up the stairs toward the locker room, I calmly asked Alex to come in so that I could talk to him.

"Alex, you know the rule. You were late, so Jaime is going to start tonight. If he does well, he will continue to play. If he screws up, I'll put you in."

He stared at me in disbelief and anger. I continued, "I can't lie to myself and I can't lie to you guys. I say what I mean and I mean what I say. I can't be a phony. I wouldn't ask you to be a phony either. Now, you're still a member of this team and next week, you'll still be the starter... unless you're late again. I expect you to be unselfish and accept the consequence for your actions. Now, go get your gear and get ready to go."

I didn't give Alex a chance to reply and I don't think he would have said anything, anyway. He slowly walked out the door, grabbed his shoulder pads and helmet that he had placed on the stairs, and shuffled his way to the locker room. I thought to myself, "Jaime better play his ass off tonight. If we lose because of him, my butt's in a ringer. Coach will kill me!"

Jaime had an incredible game! He made fourteen tackles, had two sacks and forced a fumble as we beat the blazes out of Dominguez. As soon as the game was over, I walked up to Alex and told him that I was proud of him for being a man and accepting his punishment. I also told him that he was now the starter, and it was his job to either keep or give away.

Alex changed after that night. He hustled during drills at practice and listened whenever I corrected his mistakes on the field. I didn't get any more of his cold stares as he listened intently to what I told him. As Alex's attitude improved, so did our defense and team. We played better and we were on a roll. Three weeks after I benched him, we played our crosstown rival in another league game. They were not very good, so I think our team took them lightly. This resulted in our opponent taking a big lead into the locker room at halftime.

Players always entered the locker room first during halftime to get water and use the restroom before coaches entered to address them. Our coaches met outside to discuss what we needed to adjust for the second half before entering to talk to the players. There was a difference this night. Coach Mahlstede was fuming as we stood outside the locker room. He was furious because it was obvious that our team was not playing with the intensity he expected of them. After the coaches talked for a while, Coach Mahlstede just stood there and didn't move.

"Coach, are you gonna go talk to them?" I asked.

"Hell no!" he snorted. "They don't care! It's obvious! They need to get their butts ready to play. I have nothing to tell them!"

This was unusual, so I asked again, "Coach, don't you think you need to tell them that?"

"No! It's up to them! It's their damn team, and they need to fix it themselves!"

All the coaches just stood there, looking at each other, not knowing what to say or do. Finally, I asked Coach Mahlstede, "Can I talk to them?"

"Do whatever you want, LaVigne!" With that, I walked into the locker room to talk to the players. I didn't know what exactly I would say. I just knew that they needed to hear something from their coaches.

I just had my wisdom teeth taken out a couple days earlier, and I still had the stitches in my mouth, making me sound like an old, mumbling Mafia guy who couldn't enunciate his words. I could barely speak, but I walked in and jumped on top of the lockers to implore them to get their heads and hearts back into the game. I didn't have any technical offensive or defensive adjustments to give them. I just called them all together and went on a rant, sharing the extreme displeasure of Coach Mahlstede as well as the fact that, if these crosstown guys beat us that night, they would "own us" for an entire year. I was as animated and intense as I have ever been with a team before or since.

As I spoke to them, I got more and more worked up and I could feel the stitches popping in my mouth. I continued on my frenzied rant and could feel blood running down my face. Their eyes got wide as they watched me challenge them as blood dripped from my mouth. It must have been a sight! I was positive but I didn't hold back as I let out everything I was feeling. I told them that they were better than this and that they had complete control over what would happen in the second half. The emotion and intensity in the room were obvious, as their wide eyes were joined by curled lips and looks of determination. I jumped down off the lockers when I finished and walked out the door as I yelled, "Now let's go out and punish these bastards!"

The room erupted and the players charged past me and the other coaches as they sprinted to the field. Alex was leading the pack and he had fire in his eyes. Coach Mahlstede noticed that and decided to use Alex in his sometimes role as running back. Alex responded by breaking tackles, running over opposing players, and gaining about 150 yards in that second half. He also played like a demon possessed on defense, making big play after big play. When the dust settled and the horn sounded to end the game, we knew that we played with passion and showed our opponents, the people in the stands, and ourselves who we really were.

To be honest, I don't even remember if we won that game. What I do remember is that I was so proud of these guys that I couldn't contain myself. I also couldn't talk because my mouth hurt like Hell! After the game, players were embracing each other and nodding to each other, realizing that they had played to their potential. I walked up to Alex and told him that he had one Hell of a game. He just looked at me and squinted his eyes and smiled as he gave me a big hug. He had never hugged me before. Hell, I had never seen him hug anyone before, so I was filled with emotion. It was a moment I will never forget.

We finished the regular season and got into the playoffs. That was the good news. The bad news was that we were scheduled to play Loyola at their stadium in the first round. That same team that we scrimmaged months earlier had gotten better and better and was now nationally ranked. We watched them on film during the days preceding our game, and it was obvious that we had a monumental challenge ahead of us. They were big, quick, disciplined, and very talented. They looked like a machine as we watched them on film destroy every opponent they faced. We were in for a fight.

In the locker room before the game, players paced and stared straight ahead as they readied themselves for battle. The air was thick with passion and focused intensity as I called my linemen into a shower area to talk to them and reassure them that they were more than ready to shock our seemingly invincible opponent. The call for "early outs" came, when our kickers, punters, long snappers, and returners joined other "skill position players" taking the field for warm ups. Within twenty minutes, the linemen would join them to stretch as a team and get ready for kickoff.

Linemen are not considered "skill players" but are the big guys up front who engage in a continual series of "controlled street fights" that determine who will and will not run for first downs and touchdowns. Ours is the more primitive, basic element of football that boils down to brute force, technique, and the will to attack the guy in front of you for a bigger cause. We were ready when a loud voice from another assistant coach yelled, "Okay, men. It's time!"

During the time in the locker room and throughout the game, the loudest, most dominant voice of encouragement came from Alex. He pounded on the shoulder pads of his teammates as he stared them in the eye, telling them, "Let's go kick their ass! C'mon, man, let's DO this!" It was amazing to see this but even more amazing to see Alex on the field, helping teammates up after plays, slapping their butts with encouragement, and holding his fist in the air as he inspired everyone around him in the moments before each play. It was a heroic effort and an incredible transformation in a young man who, only a few short months earlier, could care less about anyone but himself.

Our team fought their hearts out that night. We lost in a close game by a single touchdown, but even as a young, inexperienced coach, I realized that I had the great blessing of seeing a much bigger victory. Alex found the path that led him to understand that he was accountable to every member of his team, that in order to truly contribute to that greater cause, he had to give up a part of himself. I just hope that he will never forget that lesson for the rest of his life.

35

WONDER

"Wonder is the beginning of wisdom."

~ Socrates

ARIANA, BIANCA, AND VICTORIA

I constantly tell my students to look beyond the moment, day, week, and even year to see what their lives can be and embrace the wonder of what the world has to offer. I give them examples of others who had the courage and vision needed to relentlessly overcome seemingly insurmountable circumstances to realize their dreams. Three of my students gave me the best example I would ever need to share with future classes.

Ariana, one of my most challenging students, turned the corner on what had been a tumultuous life toward one that is now framed in her determination to work hard for a better future more than the ugly past that she sadly had to endure as a young child. Her parents each spent alternating stints in jail while the other cared for her in deplorable conditions, shuffling from one hotel room to the next, one step ahead of the rent-collecting landlords. Sometimes, the change of residences required Ariana to sleep in a car because there was simply not enough money to pay for a room, let alone a mortgage or monthly rent for an apartment. There were periods when both parents were imprisoned, and Ariana fell into the care of a relative who was not in a much better situation. She had seen it all—dark streets with loud, drunken, threatening voices that permeated the night air. She had never been given the security and safety that every child deserves and needs, and her defiant attitude was a natural consequence of her past.

Somehow, Ariana found hope and direction. She listened to our lessons of perseverance and was encouraged by her mentor's patient help. Her eyes began to soften, and she began to change. Her transformation was initially gradual but exploded in a singular dedication as she began her junior year of high school. Ariana became a great student and a caring person. She started to encourage others, even her close friends with whom she had once partied in drunken releases from her grim reality. She spent time in my classroom during morning break and at lunchtime, completing her assignments as she sipped the broth from her Cup-of-Noodles and nibbled on cookies. When she became aware of a student who was struggling in a particularly bad situation, she sought that kid out, helping him or her with homework or simply listening as that student tearfully spoke of the challenges being faced. Ariana became a dynamic support to others as well as an outstanding student herself.

Edgar Ulloa, a great guidance counselor at La Serna, discovered an opportunity for students who overcame adversity to excel in school. It was a national award and scholarship offered every semester by a company, *Club Z! In-Home Tutoring*. We were told it was the largest in-home tutoring company in the country. He sent an email to all of our teachers, asking us to nominate anyone we thought was deserving of this award. I nominated several of my students who had achieved great things in spite of tremendous adversity, but I felt that our best applicant was Ariana.

My expectations were not very high, however, because this was an award for the spring semester, one that only six students in the entire country would receive. I knew that Ariana deserved this honor, but I had nominated some students in the fall, and Bianca, one of our incredible seniors, had been selected for this national recognition. Bianca had also overcome extreme adversity in her personal life to achieve great success as a student. The chances were slim that another La Serna student would be selected with so many nominees throughout the country.

A few weeks after submitting my nominations, I received an email that knocked my socks off. Ariana had been chosen as one of the six national recipients of this award and scholarship. Holy moly! I was so excited that I couldn't sit or stand still. I called Edgar to confirm Ariana's selection, and then waited for her to come to my third period class where Mr. Ulloa would announce this achievement to her as well as to the entire class of students and mentors.

Could this be true? I looked at the email again, reviewing the list of award winners. There was a student from Oregon and one from Wyoming. I carefully examined the list, seeing another name from Missouri and another from Florida. Then, I saw Ariana's name again, and I just stared at it in disbelief.

What was even more amazing was that, not only had both Bianca and Ariana been selected from the same school, but they were in the same class, third period, and Bianca was Ariana's academic mentor! The judges didn't know this because I never mentioned it in either girl's nomination. The fact that they both received this honor and a $500.00 scholarship was one of the most incredible things I've ever seen happen.

When the announcement was made in class, Ariana's eyes shined bright and her broad smile showed her pride and something even more important. Ariana received a clear and strong message: hard work, dedication, and unselfish compassion lead to great things. She was on cloud nine for days, and it couldn't have happened to a more deserving, extraordinary person!

Before we knew it, the next year was upon us and I was asked once again to nominate a student for this award. I thought to myself, "There's no way that one of our students would win again, but I nominated a very special girl, Victoria, anyway.

Victoria also had to endure a childhood that is unthinkable for most people to even imagine. Both of her parents were drug addicts and alcoholics. For the first four years of her life, Victoria lived mostly on the streets with aimless, addicted parents who neglected and abused her. After I got to know her well and she accepted what we were preaching, she used to tell me about her memories of being ordered by her parents to beg from strangers and dig through the contents of trash bins to find food or anything else of use to her and her repulsive parents. This continued until her aunt rescued and adopted her. Her aunt tried to erase all these horrible memories as well as the pain they caused this beautiful little girl, but it didn't come easy.

Victoria never seemed to fit in with the other students in school. The laughter and the feeling of being safe that all children deserve evaded her for many years. She was angry, defiant, untrusting, and detached. Teachers struggled with her behavior, and fellow students learned to avoid her. She continued, year after year, to simply survive with no true sense of self-worth or direction. Then, she ended up in our classroom.

It was not easy for her to trust anyone, let alone some old, quirky teacher and an academic mentor with whom she had nothing in common. For months, she seemed to ignore us as we greeted her with smiles and gave her all the patience and encouragement we knew how to give. We found out, though, that she had not been totally ignoring us. She was just testing us. Was this compassion real or just another thing that would let her down?

Our consistency paid off, and Victoria began to listen. She even smiled from time to time. Her smiles evolved to occasional laughter as she shared stories with her mentor and classmates. Well into her sophomore year of high school, Victoria realized that this newfound devotion was real, and that's all it took.

Victoria began doing her work in class and actually brought completed homework to us, showing that she was trying. Our pride in her and all of our praise seemed to ignite her desire to do more as a student. Her F's became D's and then they became C's and B's. She finished the second semester with all A's and B's, basking in the warmth of people who truly believed in her and who deeply cared. The squinty-eyed looks of distrust were replaced with the face of a beautiful girl who was finally able to experience the love, devotion, and safety that she had been denied so many years before.

Victoria began her junior year as a totally different person than she was a year earlier. She was a serious student, concentrating and working hard in class. She not only passed her classes; she excelled in them! She also became a leader, helping others who didn't understand how to do a problem in math or struggled with identifying the underlying conditions that led to some historical event. She would lead groups in preparing oral presentations and calmly, compassionately listen to classmates who were going through their own personal Hell. She was electric, and it was an amazing thing to witness! Her impressive new attitude also led me to ask for her help.

She was a TA (teacher's assistant) during another period in the day, something I encourage certain students to do so that I am able to keep an eye on them. These TA's complete some tasks for me, but the great majority of their time is spent on their own work, keeping them on-task. In this class, however, I had a student who had exasperated me. His name was Nathan. Nathan had gone through several mentors who were all unable to get him to do any of his work. He was not angry or confrontational. He was simply not interested in anything related to school. He would simply sit, smile, and do nothing all period long. Repeated efforts to engage him, including switching his mentors who all gave him their very best, never led to a change in him. I was at the end of my rope, so I asked Victoria if she could help him to figure things out. She enthusiastically agreed and became Nathan's next and final academic mentor.

Victoria sat in the back of the room with Nathan and exhibited an incredible amount of patience in working with him on a daily basis. It was common for her to step outside the classroom with him and have a private conversation that was, no doubt, more like a counseling session. After several minutes, they would return to class, and I would notice Nathan actually working on assignments. This continued and eventually, this aimless imp became a pretty darn good student. He showed up to school every day and even began combing his big, bushy head of blond hair. Occasionally, he would still try to roam the class, seeking out anyone who might be willing to chat about a new video game or song. Victoria would soon follow him, directing Nathan back to his seat where she attentively watched over him as he completed schoolwork.

Victoria would even meet him in my class during nutrition and lunch periods to give Nathan extra help. The results were astonishing! Nathan passed all of his classes and would eventually graduate a year after Victoria.

I included all of this information as well as Victoria's own remarkable transformation on her nomination for this national academic award and was completely shocked when I received an email from *Club Z! In-Home Tutoring*: "We want to congratulate you and Victoria Alonso on her selection as one of our six national scholarship award winners…." I was floored! I knew that she deserved this honor but also knew the tremendous odds against her receiving it. She was the third consecutive student from our school to be named as a recipient of this national honor. This had never happened before, and I was elated.

I carefully read the rest of the email over and over, looking closely to see where the other honorees lived: Pennsylvania, Kansas, Texas, New Hampshire, and Ohio. "Holy Lord! This is unbelievable!" I thought to myself.

Victoria was so proud when the representative from *Club Z! In-Home Tutoring* came to school and presented a huge six-foot-long check to her! (Victoria also received a regular sized check that she could cash and deposit but she liked the big one the most!) The class cheered as the presentation was made. Our principal, some administrators, and counselors came to our classroom to witness the event and took a photo with Victoria holding that gigantic check. It was the happiest day of her life.

These three girls, Bianca, Ariana, and Victoria, completed a cycle of success that was pure magic. It filled them with joy and gave them confidence, empowering them to continue on their road of dreams and wonder. Their story and achievement also gave this old teacher the best possible example to share with future students, urging them to dream big and never give up.

36

LOVE

"Being deeply loved by someone gives you strength,
while loving someone deeply gives you courage."

~ Lao Tzu

RICK

When a teacher mentions the word "love" to his teenage students, they inevitably roll their eyes and give each other "Oh! You gotta be kidding me" looks to each other. Some giggle and others just shake their heads. Many, if not most, of them immediately think of romantic love that permeates their consciousness as hormones run amok in their adolescent lives. When an old teacher starts telling his students that there are many different kinds of love that are all powerful and meaningful, they squirm uncomfortably in their seats, anticipating some sappy sermon about a topic they would prefer not to discuss. I have come to expect that reaction when I broach this core value with my students. I am actually amused by their understandable reaction.

Sadly, many of my students get a paltry portion of love in their lives. They are often ignored by their parents, ridiculed by classmates, and neglected by others who are too wrapped up in their own lives to realize what they are missing. Many of my students have families that suffer from the absence of real love in their homes due to things like drugs, abandonment, and a variety of other reasons. That absence of love and its nurturing encouragement is what leads many young people to seek that basic human need in other, potentially destructive ways. Some of these kids don't even believe that there is such a thing as unselfish, committed love. Some just don't know what to think. It was nice to unknowingly, give them a great example.

One day during class, my phone rang. As my students were quietly busy doing some independent work, I answered. It was a call from Rick Leon, a young man I coached almost twenty years before. He is very special to me for many reasons. He is a great human being who has always been fiercely loyal to me. When he played football for me, I learned that his father lived far away and had not been a big part of his life. I seemed to somehow fill that void for him, and we became very close. I often introduce him to others as my third son, and he is like a big brother to both Clint and Mark. He coached for me at La Serna for several years when I first arrived. He also honored me with a tremendous gift, giving his first son the middle name of Ken... after me. Rick was raised by his mother with the constant presence and support of his grandfather, Robert. Rick's son is named Robert Ken Leon. It is an honor that makes me proud every time I think about it.

Rick is also very thoughtful and calls me, my wife, and our two sons on our birthdays. That means a lot. He was calling that morning to wish me Happy Birthday. What a great person he is! In addition to making me feel good, his call had a big impact on my students as they listened to my end of the telephone conversation.

"Thanks, Rick. I appreciate that. How's Christina? And Robbie? How about Logan and Noah? How are they doin'?"

"Yes, Gisele and the boys are doing fine. They miss seeing you. We're gonna come down and visit you soon."

"Thank you, Rick. I love you, too! Take care. I can't wait to see you and the family. Goodbye."

As I hung up, I saw my students just staring at me. "Who was that?" they asked.

I explained that it was a very special young man who was once one of my kids, just like them. I told them I hoped I would get calls from them someday and get a chance to share their lives when they were older.

They were quiet and a bit stunned, continuing to stare at me. Then someone said, "You really *do* love your students, don't you, Mr. LaVigne?"

"I sure do!" I said, "And don't ever forget it!"

37

HOPE

"Hope is the thing with feathers
That perches in the soul
And sings the tune without the words
And never stops at all."

~ Emily Dickinson

EUGENE

Hope is a powerful thing. It sustains us in times of deep despair as we grapple with disillusionment and heartache. Sometimes, hope seems futile and foolish, but we hold tight to it, anyway, simply because it is the only thing that gets us through dark and daunting circumstances. This was especially true for a young man named Eugene.

Eugene entered my class as a sophomore with an outward appearance that belied his true life's situation. He was a chubby, round-faced kid with freckles and short blond hair that was neatly combed with a straight part down the side of his head. He had a smile that was simultaneously happy, engaging, and mischievous. He dressed modestly and conservatively with no hints of gang affiliation. He just seemed like a normal kid.

As time went by in class, he revealed much more of himself. He failed most of his classes the previous year, and it was easy to see why. He was constantly distracted, seeking the attention of classmates much more than concentrating on his schoolwork. He could be charming and in the next instant, defiant and disrespectful. His propensity to arrive to class late without his notebook or homework drove me crazy as did his apparent inability to focus on anything for more than thirty seconds. He was a handful, and we had many private talks that shed light on his real-life situation.

Eugene lived alone with his grandmother. His father was in prison, serving a life sentence for murder, and his mother was a meth addict, appearing in his life only occasionally to make promises that she almost never kept. Another fact that must have been drilled deeply in his brain and heart was that his grandmother had terminal cancer and little resources to battle her condition. Eugene and his grandmother scraped by with what they had, and it was evident that Eugene's spirit was lost in his own dire reality. It was terribly sad and difficult to hear these things about a kid who had no control over so much adversity that he had to face. Hope was one of my strongest tools in my attempt to straighten out his tangled life.

I hoped for a change in him and some inspiration that would lead him to build a happy and successful future. He hoped for a way out but sought his release with apathy and the simple, understandable detachment that would tempt anyone in his situation. It was a long and frustrating first year with Eugene. He never quite embraced what I was selling and did not respond to the efforts of his well-intentioned mentor. He continued to fail classes and act out in class. All of our attempts to turn him around often seemed futile. All we could do was hope, pray, and give him all the love and support possible. By the end of his sophomore year, despite everything we tried, it was apparent that Eugene was simply not improving. Not to punish him but to give him his best chance to graduate high school, his counselor had no choice but to send him to continuation school in the hope that he would somehow find success in its alternative program. To be honest, I had my doubts, lots of them.

I was shocked when he appeared in my classroom at the beginning of his senior year. He was not the pudgy kid anymore. He had grown taller and leaner but still had that engaging smile that was less mischievous and more determined. I was sitting at my desk, grading papers when he approached tentatively. He had a permission slip from the guidance office in his hands, requesting my approval for him to be my TA in one of my classes. I put down my pen and removed my glasses as I noticed him walking toward me.

"Mr. LaVigne, I'm back. I finally figured it out. I passed all my classes at continuation school and now I'm back here to graduate."

"Really? Wow! That's so great to hear, Eugene! Are you sure that you have all your credits?"

He looked at me with his big smile and said, "Yea. I even finished enough classes to be your TA if you'll let me."

"Are you kidding? Of course I'll let you! I'd love to have you, but I have to tell you something. I can't accept any more of the "old Eugene" attitude. I'm going to make sure you work and I expect you to finish this thing and graduate. Do you understand that?"

"Yea, I do," he said as he once again gave me that big smile of his.

"Okay," I said as I signed his permission slip. "I expect you to come to class every day with work to do. Your other schoolwork takes priority over anything I need you to do as my TA. I just want you to graduate. Got it?"

"Yup! Sure do!

With that, he left. I sat there, staring straight ahead, wondering if he really would follow through and hoping with all my heart that he would. He didn't disappoint himself or me. He came to class on time every day and worked hard on his assignments. He would occasionally ask for help on some project or other homework sheet, and I was always happy to jump in there with him. I could see that he was serious and motivated now so after several weeks, I asked him, "What happened over there that made such a difference in you? I'm very proud of you now, but I'd love to know what changed things for you."

"I didn't like it where I was. I wanted to be back here, and I remembered what you told me about nothing changing unless I did. I finally decided to change. That's all."

"Well, I'm happy as a clam that you did!"

"What do you mean 'Happy as a clam'?"

"Never mind. It's just a saying that really fits right now." I smiled at my old-fashioned mind and at his complete change of heart.

Eugene finished his senior year with us, earning no grade lower than a C. Graduation day was special that year. It always is, but Eugene's life change made it especially gratifying. My graduation day assignment is to check all the seniors in at our gym and make sure they get on the bus to the stadium for the ceremony. There are excited, relieved faces everywhere as our seniors walk around, chatting with their classmates as they hug each other and share high-fives. After everyone has been checked in and right before we board the buses, I get on the microphone and ask all of our OASIS graduates to meet me at a certain spot to take our final group photo that I proudly display in my classroom. There is complete frenzy in that room with kids deeply engaged in conversations they don't want to end, so getting them together is like herding kittens.

Finally, all the kids gathered about me for the picture. In the weeks before graduation day, Eugene was worried about not having the required shirt, tie, dress pants, and dress shoes that are required of all our graduates. His grandmother really didn't have the money to spend on that, so I bought a gift card at J.C. Penney and gave it to him to get what he needed. He was so proud in his new outfit but he did not have his tie on. That was the first time he had worn all of his new clothes together. He sheepishly called me over to him and asked, "Mr. LaVigne, will you tie my tie?"

It was the second time in my life that one of my students melted my heart with that request. I smiled widely as I reached out for the tie. I wrapped it around my own neck and tied a Half-Windsor and handed it back to him. He struggled with it so I helped him secure it under his collar, straightening it out as I reminded him of what a special person he was and how proud of him that I was. Once again, he shot that smile back at me and seemed to glow. We lined up and took the photo and then assembled the grads in another line as I counted them off to board the buses.

When Eugene got to the front of the line, he stopped and stared at me. He had tears in his eyes and his mouth was trembling as he said, "Mr. LaVigne, thank you! This is the best day of my life!"

"The first of many more to come, my friend! Now go enjoy your moment. You sure deserve it!"

One last smile, and Eugene joined his friends as they walked toward a bus ride and a whole new life. I hope he has a great one.

38

COURAGE, CHARACTER, AND COMMITMENT

"Courage. Character. Commitment.
That's what we're going to be all about.
These are the things that will make us champions."

~ Ken LaVigne
(The first words I said to my new team at the last
school I would ever coach)

COACH DAVE AND COACH ANDY

Coming to my new school, as the head varsity football coach, was exciting but very difficult. I left my old school as an assistant to the man who changed my life. We were very successful there, and I loved and enjoyed everything and everyone I was leaving; yet, I knew that this was something I had to do. I saw the window closing on my coaching career and knew that I would never be satisfied with myself if I did not take on the challenge of leading a football program as its head coach one final time. I spent ten great years as a coach there, winning some games but more importantly, influencing some lives in a way I never could have done as an assistant.

Years have passed, and I have been fulfilled beyond description in my new role as a teacher of at-risk kids. I have also been lucky because of the way former players and coaches have accepted me, making me feel that I am still an important part of what they do. Two coaches have had an especially significant effect on me in the years since I have coached.

*

Dave Pierson coached alongside me at my former school and joined me at my new one. He is a talented, dedicated coach with tremendous character. After many years on my staff, he left to become the head coach at a small high school that had never had any real success in football. His first years were very tough as his teams struggled against others with greater numbers and better athletes. He remained strong in his conviction there, and it wasn't that long before his teams were very successful. We spoke often on the phone, sharing ideas and memories together. I always enjoyed and appreciated those phone calls.

Toward the end of one of his successful seasons, he called and invited Gisele and me to his game, the first home playoff game his school had ever hosted. My wife and I excitedly accepted his invitation and attended that game. Rebecca, Dave's wonderful wife, met us at the gate and led us to where she and other wives of coaches were seated in the stands.

Then she told me, "Ken, Dave wants you on the sideline with him." She pointed to the sidelines, and I saw Dave there, waving at me to come join him. I did, and when I got there, he gave me a

Jaguars football tee shirt and a game program. I thanked him, and he smiled as he said, "Look at the cover of the program, Coach." I looked at the program and saw **Courage, Character, Commitment** printed in large block letters on the cover. We both smiled and hugged as my eyes started to water. "Dave, you honor me and make me very proud," I said as I blinked over and over to get rid of the tears that filled my eyes. He just smiled and said, "Coach, it's what I believe."

A few years later, he was named as the new head coach at Santa Fe, our old school, replacing the coaching legend and man who had been my life's greatest mentor. I called and congratulated him, and he told me that we needed to get together after he got settled. I happily agreed. A few months later, he called and said that we should have lunch together. We settled on a day and time during the summer and met at the school. We went to have lunch and when we returned to school, he told me that he wanted to show me something.

Dave led me to the team room. We walked down the stairs I had walked thousands of times before and entered the room. It was just as I remembered it except for one big difference. There was a huge conference table in the middle of the room that was obviously intended for staff and player group meetings. "Look at the table closely, Coach. Look at the sides."

Beautifully carved on the sides of this enormous table where his coaches and players would meet were the words **Courage, Character, and Commitment**. I stared at the words for a long while before looking up to see my friend's smiling face, beaming back at me. "Pretty cool, huh Coach," he said.

"Very cool, David!" I said as I shook my head in amazement.

*

Andy George was one of my assistant coaches at La Serna for several years. He had been a tremendous football player while in high school, and actually played on an all-star team that I coached after his senior year. He is a dedicated and caring man who is now the head varsity coach at La Serna. I like and respect Andy very much. He is an excellent coach and an even better man. He makes me feel comfortable and welcome as a frequent guest on the sidelines of his games. His love for his players is evident and his impact on them is obvious as I watch him calmly direct his team with strength and genuine passion.

After major back surgery and a total ankle reconstruction in the past few years, it is difficult for me to walk the long distance from the parking lot to the stadium. Andy knows this and allows me to ride on the bus with the team. I sit quietly and watch the intense determination on the faces of his players as they travel to the stadium and compete during the games. It is a real joy and honor to do this, but Andy gave me something special before one of these games.

On the morning of an important league game, Andy called me in my classroom. "You're going to ride the bus with us tonight, aren't you, Coach?"

"Yes, if it's okay, Andy. Is everything alright?"

"Yea, everything's fine, Coach. I just wanted to make sure that you'll be coming. I have a surprise for you."

I had no idea what he was talking about and to be honest, I forgot all about this "surprise" as we rode to the game on the bus. I was fixated on the players and coaches, taking in the intense atmosphere of the team on the bus. When we arrived at the stadium, Andy made sure to have me walk with him toward the sideline. He quietly smiled as we stepped onto the field as he said, "Look at the press box, Coach." I looked up and saw an enormous banner stretching across the entire length of the press box with the words *La Serna Football* and *Courage, Character, and Commitment*. It was a permanent banner that Andy assured me would be displayed at all of our home games.

That truly touched my heart, and I said, "I am really honored by this, Coach. Thank you."

"That's who we are, Coach, and that's what we stand for."

I just kept thanking Andy while I gazed up at that banner and wondered how I ever got to be so lucky. What Andy George did means the world to me because of how important these values are and how special I feel to still be accepted as a part of the football program by its current very special head coach. Andy still asks me to attend his awards banquet every year, and there is an award given to the player who best exemplifies these qualities. Rich Ruiz, one of La Serna's great assistant coaches, called me at home on an evening before a recent awards banquet, asking me about what I felt these words mean. I shared my thoughts with him and was again honored and humbled when Coach Ruiz shared those thoughts with the hundreds of people who attended the event. I have never felt more a part of the program than at that moment.

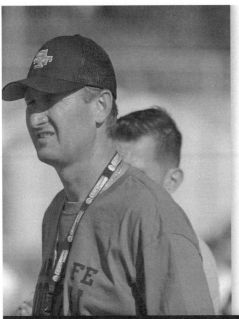

Dave Pierson
Head Varsity
Football Coach
Santa Fe
High School

Andy George
Head Varsity
Football Coach
La Serna
High School

Here's what I told Coach Ruiz and what he shared with everyone at the awards banquet. It is what I told all my football players for many years.

COURAGE is doing the right thing, even when you know that it will make you unpopular or uncomfortable. It means standing up for someone who is being picked on by others. It is being respectful in class while all your friends are making your teacher's life miserable. Courage is confronting your biggest fear, your greatest challenge with relentless conviction and never ever giving up. Courage is realizing your own weaknesses but never using them as excuses.

CHARACTER is what you do when no one is watching. It is giving your absolute best effort in school and on the field even when you realize that it might not be noticed or might not be enough. Character is working in a family-owned store where there is no camera to watch you and NEVER taking money from the cash register. It is giving back money when a store clerk mistakenly gives you too much change. Character is working as hard as you possibly can when your coach is not looking. It is making decisions every day that will bring honor and not shame to your family. It is living your life with integrity.

COMMITMENT is more than a promise because promises can and often are broken. Commitment is an uncompromising, unwavering pledge to others who depend upon you that is kept no matter what. Commitment is speaking up for your friend when others are talking about him behind his back. It is helping your family, providing everything you can to make them proud and their lives better. Commitment is being positive, tenacious, and supportive when things are looking bleak, when the odds are stacked against you. Commitment is being true to your word and to those you love.

39

GRATITUDE

*"When we give cheerfully and accept gratefully,
everyone is blessed."*

~ Maya Angelou

MEMORIES

I am very, very grateful for many things: my wife, sons, parents, friends, health, and all the people who have influenced and shaped my life. I am thankful for the beautiful memories I have of teaching and coaching for so many years. I live a charmed life that has been blessed in thousands of ways. My own gratitude is magnified by the words of my former students and players who share their hearts with me in beautiful letters that tell of their own growth. The warmth and sincerity of their messages inspire and motivate me. I always feel somewhat embarrassed by these expressions of gratitude because I know that I got a lot more than I gave.

Standing in my classroom, I can't help but stare at all the photographs of happy, successful kids who had, not too long ago, not even imagined the tremendous accomplishments that were ahead of them. I reread notes from loving students tacked on my walls and look at all the little gifts and mementos that they gave me to commemorate special, life-changing moments in their lives. I remember messages slipped to me by kids whose vision of themselves had expanded big enough to house dreams that they didn't even realize were possible just months before.

My mind drifts to Santino telling me to "just calm down and relax" as he shuffled his way to a diploma. I remember the faces of frightened, insecure souls who struggled with their sexuality and the constant threat of exposure and ridicule. I see happy faces and high-fives given by mentors to their students who just received their tests with big A's written on them in red ink. I relive long talks with students outside my room filled with tears and anguish as we share a box of tissues to wipe our eyes. I hear the desperate voices of parents who have called me, crying and begging me to help their little girl or little boy. My mind is like a bulletin board with countless tacks, attaching notes of both successes and failures. I remember students who have made me so angry that I had to stop in front of my class and turn away for a minute or two until I was able to gather myself and regain my composure. I see and feel and hear these things every day as I walk around my class, cajoling and encouraging my students like a cheerleader on the sideline of a football game. These are memories of sadness and joy, but mostly, they are reminders that what these kids need most is someone to laugh and cry with them and above all else, believe in them.

I think about Juliana's beautiful note to me after our field trip to UCLA.

> *"Mr. LaVigne, before our field trip, I didn't even know that a place like this existed until we went there. I love that college so much! I'm going to go there. I promise! I know it will take a lot of work and dedication, but I'm ready for all of that. Thanks for giving me a dream and teaching what I need to get it."*

Now, that's a hell of a note!

40

WIN: WHAT'S IMPORTANT NOW

"The reason most people never reach their goals is that they don't define them, learn about them, or even seriously consider them as believable or achievable. Winners can tell you where they are going, what they plan to do along the way, and who will be sharing the adventure with them."

~ Denis Waitley

CHARLIE

During the spring, a few of our teachers have their students write letters to people who had made a difference in their lives. This practice always gives me precious reading material and more beautiful notes to place in my "keeper file", a large box where I keep extra special messages from students that I intend to read over and over again when I am retired. One of these letters came from Charlie, a tough-looking senior with whom I really struggled as a sophomore and junior. Charlie looked like he could be the model for a dirt bike riding magazine: slender, muscular, and grizzled. He had the look of someone who could tear your head off if you looked at him the wrong way. He missed a lot of school as both a sophomore and junior but always rallied at the last possible moment, saving his grades and his chances of graduating. That habit of many absences and procrastination made me worry about him after his junior year when I wouldn't see him every day. Once again, I was wrong in my evaluation, and he became a stellar student as a senior.

I'm not a weird "cat guy" who goes crazy with adopting too many of these creatures in some strange obsession, but I do like the feline population a lot. Cats are, in my eyes, majestic creatures whose natural characteristics resemble those of teenagers. They are beautiful but fiercely independent and not given to being tamed. If you feed them, they will return, but only on their terms. If you are patient enough and don't push too hard, they grow to trust you.

Charlie always reminded me of a tough feral cat who, despite constant wounds from fights and a mysterious ability to exist without a stable home, persisted and survived. He also kept coming back to school, even without the stability of a normal home life, exhibiting different wounds that came from neglect. I hoped the best for him, but I knew better than to completely trust that he would continue to return and prevail. That is why his letter to me at the end of his senior year was so touching and gratifying.

Dear Mr. LaVigne,

Throughout my years of high school, my sophomore and junior years affected me the most in a good way, only because you taught me many very good skills to use. I began my sophomore year in a very deep hole, and you were always the one to throw me a ladder and help me when I needed the help the most. You always taught us to WIN "What's Important Now" with the advice you always gave me. I took every word you said to me and turned it into something good. I mean, can't you tell that you are the reason that I have a 3.0 grade point average? Every assignment I have, if I get lazy, you pop into my head and all that amazing advice you've given me has helped me so much, Mr. LaVigne. I am very thankful for all you've done for me and all your other students. You have really changed my views on life, and I really appreciate all that you have done. Thank you, Mr. LaVigne. I love you like a father. I really do!

> *Sincerely,*
> *Charlie Hancock*

I have received more eloquently written letters, but none any more meaningful and beautiful than Charlie's. I made sure to tell him so. When he appeared in his cap and gown on graduation day, I couldn't control my joy and pride in him. I gave him one last bit of truth that I wanted him to keep inside him forever, "Charlie, what I gave you is nothing compared to everything you gave me. Thank you!" With that, he gave me a hug and walked away, celebrating his great achievement of beating the odds stacked against him.

41

AWARENESS

"What lies behind us and what lies before us are tiny matters compared to what lies within us."

~Henry Stanley Haskins

OSCAR

I looked up from my desk and saw Oscar standing in front of me, just a few weeks before graduation. He told me about his senior project and the presentation he had prepared. His excitement was real and genuine. My mind slipped back to when I first met him at the end of his freshman year. Highly intelligent but with a fiercely independent spirit, he'd wince at the mention of an assignment that was due the next day, telling me, "That assignment's stupid. I don't need to do that! I know all the stuff that we covered. Why do I have to do all this ridiculous stuff?" I remember telling him it was because it is part of the process and a necessary step he had to take. He reluctantly complied, but he continued to challenge the validity of a hundred things he felt were juvenile and absurd.

Now, Oscar was standing in front of me, telling me how sorry he was for giving me such a hard time when he started with us in our program. He also thanked me. "Mr. LaVigne, at first, I thought all the stuff you did was really dumb and weird. I know that I fought you, but you stayed patient with me. Now I know why you said all the things you did and why we did all those activities. I finally got it, and it's why I'm graduating. Thank you, Mr. LaVigne. I'll never forget you."

Not many days later, Oscar graduated. His long black hair looked good riding under his graduation cap as he made his final exit from La Serna, moving on to college and his own dream of being a psychologist.

42

OPPORTUNITY

*"The Chinese use two brush strokes to write the word
'crisis.' One brush stroke stands for danger; the other
for opportunity. In a crisis, be aware of the danger—
but recognize the opportunity."*

~ John F. Kennedy

ERIC AND THE KNIFE

In June of 2014, I received an email from a young man I coached a
long time before. It had been seventeen years since I saw or talked
with him. I was deeply moved to hear from someone whose life I
was privileged enough to touch many years earlier, and I was grateful
that the memories that he had were so meaningful to him.

Dear Coach,

*Hello, my name Eric Sanchez, I'm sure you don't remem-
ber me but you were my O-line Coach at Santa Fe during*

208

the 95-97 seasons. The purpose of my email is to thank you for everything you did for me back in high school. Your teachings in my four years (especially my Jr. and Sr.) at Santa Fe of self-worth, to do what's right, and to have confidence helped me more than you can ever understand. You were and still are a role model in my life.

Back in 2001, I was a college student and owned a furniture store with my dad, but when the economy began to struggle, we sold the store to make ends meet and my family and I lost our house. I took a job at the new Target store in Norwalk so I could have money to take care of my family. But we were homeless. We lived in motels. I slept on the floor and had to worry about drug dealers and gang members trying to break into our room to do God knows what. As weeks turned into months, and months started to turn into years, I began to lose faith and started to think I was worthless.

In 2005, I came to the conclusion that I was never getting out of the hell I was in, so I decided to make a change and find a way to get my family out of this situation. Unfortunately, the only things I found were setbacks. Frustrated, I asked my best friend for a job where he worked as a last ditch effort. I also told myself that if I didn't get the job I was going to kill myself. Well, I got the job and began to slowly recover. I know that if it wasn't for you and what you taught me, I never would have made it out of those 4 years of hell my family and I went though.

I am now coaching football at South High in Torrance (going on my second year), and I am about to go back to school to get my Business degree and I have you to thank. Coach, without you entering my life at the time that you did and caring about me, taking the time to see how I was doing and just taking an interest in me, I never would have graduated from high school and I would not have been able to write you this. I hope I am able to be a fraction of the man and coach you are because if I am, then I will be able to help my kids (players) the way you helped me.

I am having a hard time finding a way to finish this letter because the truth is, I really do not want to. I will say this: I hope I have the opportunity to one day sit down with you and thank you in person. I am honored to call you my coach, my mentor, and my friend. In fact, you are family to me.

> *Thank you for everything, Coach,*
> **Eric Javier Sanchez**

I replied to Eric's email, assuring him that I remember him very well. A few weeks later, he asked to come by and see me on a rare day off from work. We went out to lunch and talked for hours, reminiscing about old times and things I had long forgotten but remembered with joy as Eric reminded me of them. He recalled things I said and did that were critical to him, but were not grand efforts on my part to provide wisdom or dispense hope. They were just things that coaches say to their players because they care about them. They emerge as game changers in kids' lives as a natural product of a relationship built on love, trust, and respect.

After lunch, Eric took me home, and we sat for a while longer in my living room, talking. He told me something that affected me profoundly. He said that, in his crossroads moment of truth, he answered the phone call from a friend that he had asked for a job. His life was so dark and hopeless, that he spoke to this friend with the phone in one hand and a knife in the other. He said that he was going to end his misery that day one way or another. If there was not a job for him and a chance for redemption in that phone call, he was going to use that knife to end his life. He said that, when he was given this opportunity of a job, he lowered the knife.

Damn! That is powerful stuff!

I'm an English teacher and I see many things in life as metaphors. That knife represented the ultimate act of desperation and loss of hope. Eric getting that job represented opportunity. From now on, I won't be able to get that image out of my mind and see the desperation of my students without hope looking back at me as I stand in front of them as their teacher. It's my job to give them what they need to drop their knives and move forward. That's a powerful image and one I plan to use to be the best teacher and source of opportunity that I can possibly be until I'm dragged out of my classroom, kicking and screaming because I'm just too damned old to do it anymore.

43

PEACE

"The Simple Path:
Silence is Prayer,
Prayer is Faith,
Faith is Love,
Love is Service,
The Fruit of Service is Peace"

~ Mother Teresa

FELIPE

A recent year was the most exhausting and challenging that I had ever experienced as a teacher. There were some uniquely difficult situations that involved volatile students who threatened, intimidated, and frightened their classmates. After careful thought and consideration of all the factors, I took steps that I was sure were necessary to ensure the safety of all my students. For the first time, however, others on whom I had always relied for support questioned and overruled my judgment and actions. This was done without even having a conversation with me, and I was hurt to the core. I decided that it was finally time for me to pack it in and retire. I even called our district office and inquired about the steps necessary to retire on short notice. I pulled out retirement papers at home, reviewed them with my wife, and was 98% sure that, within months, I would not be teaching anymore. Then three things happened that stopped me in my tracks.

One of those things involved Felipe, a senior who had been my student for three years. Felipe entered my class and our program as a sophomore with a 0.67 grade point average. He was graduating with a 3.17 grade point average. He is a quiet, friendly student who lives with his mother and younger brother in a home filled with love but struggles constantly with finances. His family came to America from Mexico, and his mother speaks only Spanish, limiting her opportunities to find a well-paying job. Felipe never complained about his family's situation, and it was difficult to tell that he was actually affected by it all that much.

To help facilitate our annual OASIS graduation photo and eliminate my stress in trying to gather everyone on Graduation Day, I made arrangements with Randy Castillo, our assistant principal, to have our kids get their caps and gowns thirty minutes before the rest of the seniors so that they could come to my classroom to take the photo and have a celebration of the event with pizza and sandwiches I ordered from a local Italian restaurant. On the day that was to occur, students began arriving with their caps and gowns, and I told them to relax, take some food, and wait for everyone to get there. Fifteen minutes into this process, Felipe appeared with a couple of his friends who had their caps and gowns. Felipe did not have his. I asked him what was going on, and he hemmed and hawed, giving me what really wasn't an answer at all. I finally realized that he did not have the money to buy his cap and gown so I reached into my wallet and gave him some money with instructions to hustle down to the gym, pick up his cap and gown, and get back as soon as he could. I told him that we would not take the picture without him in it.

He hesitated at first, seemingly embarrassed and unsure of what to do. Seeing this, I said, "Listen, Felipe. I've told you many times that I received help from my teachers with things like this when I was your age because my family didn't have much money. You're doing me a favor by letting me do this for you now. Now, get your butt down there and get back here as fast as you can! Hurry up! We'll be waiting for you!"

With the insistence of some of his friends who accompanied him, he left my classroom, returning ten minutes later with his required garb. He was the last student to get there, so we quickly assembled in the front of my room and had one of our younger mentors snap the picture. It was a great photo with Felipe proudly smiling in the back row.

The day after we took the picture, Felipe told me that his mother wanted to come to school and talk with me. I told him that I would love to talk with her. A few days later, I received a call from Juanita Garza, our attendance coordinator, during the tutorial period before lunch, telling me that Mrs. Hernandez was in her office and wanted to talk with me. I told Juanita that I would need a translator because Mrs. Hernandez only spoke Spanish. She told me that she would be happy to do it. That tutorial period is when I typically make private calls to parents, teachers, and counselors, so I had the flexibility to leave. I hustled down to the front of the school where I was greeted by Mrs. Hernandez and Mrs. Garza, who led us into a small conference room.

The meeting began with Mrs. Hernandez holding her hands as in prayer as she talked to me in Spanish with tears in her eyes. Mrs. Garza translated and shared the most beautiful, heartfelt things I had ever heard. She called me an angel and went on and on about how her son had changed during the past three years. She choked as she spoke to me with her lips quivering and tears running down her face. Within a few short minutes, Juanita and I were both crying, too. Mrs. Hernandez reached into her purse and with shaking hands, tried to give me some money to repay me for what I had given Felipe. I told her to please not do this. I said that knowing her son and being able to help him was a blessing. She reluctantly returned the money to her purse and continued her needless but wonderful praise and thanks. Finally, I said, "Juanita, please tell Mrs. Hernandez that she is making this old guy cry and to please stop." With that, I stood and hugged Mrs. Hernandez before walking away.

As I approached my classroom, I saw Felipe. He was walking quickly past me and said, "Mr. LaVigne, my mom wants to see the room."

I told him that I would love her to join us in the classroom. "Of course! Go get her."

I always keep extra food in my classroom to share with hungry students, so I prepared three plates with sandwiches and chips. I poured three glasses of cold water from the refrigerator and waited. Soon, Felipe appeared with his mother. We sat and ate as she gazed around in deep emotion and a piety that made it seem like she was in a cathedral. Felipe translated more kind, moving words from his mother as well as my insistence that it was me who was fortunate and grateful. All at once, I heard something that, for some reason, made me very emotional. It was the sound of some of my girl students, singing joyfully like angels in the back of the room. These were girls with wrecked lives that were on the mend. They were happy and safe, sharing their joy in song. I know that this sounds weird, but the entire scene was spiritual and mystical.

As lunch ended and Felipe left with his mother, I felt a strong peace settling over me. It was the kind of peace that I always encourage my students to feel when they simply do what is right. I knew that THIS is why I teach, not to satisfy adult colleagues who question my methods and judgment but to touch the hearts and souls of kids I truly love. I was touched beyond description and reassured that it was all worth it.

44

HUMILITY

"The soul is healed by being with children."

~ Fyodor Dostoyevsky

EMELIA

The day after Mrs. Hernandez's visit, Emilia, one of my sweet, beautiful, and goofy seniors, came to my classroom and told me that she had something to give me but she wanted to give it to me in private. She said, "You're too busy now in class, but I'll come back."

I said, "Okay."

Emilia came back to my classroom a few more times during the next two days and each time, she'd look at the hectic scene and tell me she would come back. Finally, she returned again and said, "Mr. LaVigne, you're *always* busy, and I need to give you something right now. Can we go outside so I can give it to you with nobody around?"

I was intrigued and kept telling her that she didn't need to give me anything as we walked outside my classroom. I told my students to behave while I was outside. Standing where we had spoken so many times in tearful private talks about her dreadful life's challenges, she slowly pulled out a letter from her pocket. She looked very serious as she began reading it to me.

Mr. LaVigne,

On behalf of my parents and from the bottom of my heart, I owe you my thank you. Thank you for being the person who affected my life and encouraged my mental and academic growth. I have never met another influence with such a kind soul as yours. I truly believe that God saw my struggles in my life and placed you in my life to help me. With that, I know you have the biggest blessings yet to come your way.

When I first moved to Whittier, I was completely intimidated. Coming from the hood, living my entire life in poverty in a broken home with immigrants, I felt I was destined to fail and work my entire life struggling just as generations had before me. But you came into my life as my teacher and my mentor and showed me that there was more to life than that. You showed me the variety of opportunities that life had to offer to someone like me. You're the only person in my life who actually saw potential in me. If it weren't for you, I wouldn't be the person I am today. You humbled my mind and shaped me into the student and person I am today.

Mr. LaVigne, I am the first person in my mom's family to cross the stage and the third person in my dad's family to actually graduate high school. I will also be the first person ever in my family to attend a university. My mom raised me the best she could, being a single teenage mother of two. So I know the amount of pride and love that my mother will have when she sees her daughter graduate from high school. I am a part of her American Dream of

coming to the United States and YOU helped me be a part
of that dream. Thank you, Mr. LaVigne, for helping me to
be a part of that dream.

Please, Mr. LaVigne, continue doing what you're doing
until you find someone as humble as yourself to substitute
for you. Thank you for being a father figure to me, and
thank you for believing in me. It means more to me than
you'll ever know.

Emilia, Class of 2017

When Emilia finished reading her letter, she slowly looked up at me with her big, beautiful, brown eyes and her lips pressed tightly together.

I stared at her in silence for a few seconds before she said, "That's the best thing I can give you, Mr. LaVigne."

"Well, that's the most beautiful thing that anyone has ever said to me. It is the best gift I have ever received. Thank you! My God, thank you!"

Her serious face melted into one that smiled at me with happy but watery eyes. "I love you, Mr. LaVigne."

A deep sense of humility filled me at that moment. I did not see myself as anything more than a lucky man who was able to be a part of something so beautiful and real. Emilia was and is a blessing beyond description.

"I love you, too, so very much!" She handed me the letter, and we hugged before she walked away, looking back to smile at me as she made her way to her class. I shook my head, wiped my eyes, and then reentered my classroom, announcing my entrance with, "Now what the heck have you crazy kids been doin' in here? Let's get to work!"

45

HONOR

"Our own heart, and not other men's opinions,
forms our true honor."

~ Samuel Taylor Coleridge

CAN'T RETIRE YET!

The day after Emilia read her letter to me, we were finishing my last class session with my juniors. We were on finals schedule, so we had an extra-long period. Suddenly, all of my juniors went outside and called me to join them. I asked, "What are we doing?"

"We want a picture of all of us with you, Mr. LaVigne."

I smiled in the middle of the group as a student from another class was recruited to take the picture over and over on different kids' cellphones. We finished and made our way inside. We had about thirty minutes left in the period. Natalia, a rough looking but gorgeous girl who had seen more than her share of wild nights and street fights in her young life, walked up to my desk and told me to

219

sit in a chair in the front of the class. "For what?" I said, "Are you guys going to throw things at me?"

"No. There are some things we want to tell you."

Then, one by one, these kids, most who had been my students for two years, stood in front of me and all their classmates and said the most wonderful, impassioned things to me that I had ever heard from so many in such a short period of time. Every student, even the ones who were petrified to speak in front of others, stood in front of me and publicly and exquisitely shared their feelings. It was incredible! I wiped my eyes and smiled at each of them as they marched in procession to give this old man a priceless gift of love and gratitude. When they had finished and the period was about to end, I stood up and told them how much they and their words meant to me. I rambled on, I'm sure, because the whole thing took me by surprise, and when they left, I regretted not being more eloquent in telling them all how important this was to me.

I wrote a letter to all of them that afternoon, expressing how much I love them all and how grateful I was to even know them. In the letter, I told them that most people never get a moment like that in their entire lives. I shared with them how honored I was in hearing words from them that I would never forget. I told them that this had been a rough year for me and that I seriously considered retiring, but that I would not retire, at least not now, because I wanted to see each and every one of them graduate. I meant it. I'm not going anywhere, at least not yet. These kids gave me the strength and clarity to realize that everything I do is for them and no one else.

I sent my letter to every one of them during class the next morning on the last day of school. Later during the day, many of them came back to my room to get one final hug and to make sure I kept my promise to come back. I won't break that promise. How could I?

Teaching is an honor, privilege, and joy beyond description. To see students' eyes light up when they understand a concept for the first time is something that lifts the spirit and fuels the drive in a teacher's heart. To see teenagers turn their backs on destructive lifestyles and embrace life-changing values is even more powerful. We teachers are the lucky ones who get the rare opportunity to impact the lives of tens and hundreds of different students every year. We do this, receiving the most precious reward of all, the trust and love of students who enter our classrooms every day.

46

BEAUTY

"The most beautiful people we have known are those who have known defeat, known suffering, known struggle, known loss, and have found their way out of the depths. These persons have an appreciation, a sensitivity, and an understanding of life that fills them with compassion, gentleness, and a deep loving concern. Beautiful people do not just happen."

~ Elisabeth Kübler-Ross

PRISCILLA

I have seen and heard many beautiful things in my life but none that captured the true essence of beauty more than the faces and stories of the students I have been fortunate enough to know. One of these faces is that of Priscilla Garcia, a young girl with the weight of the world on her shoulders when she became my student. She was a gorgeous kid with an infectious smile that gave my classroom warmth and charm. She graced us with her genuine spirit as a student, but there was always a tinge of sadness and desperation about her. She had a tendency to miss a lot of school, driving me crazy as I tried hard to understand her and get her to attend school.

Years after her graduation, she sent me this email, explaining the adversity she faced as a student. Her message described her dilemma and exposed the true depth of her beauty.

Hello, Mr. La Vigne :)

I hope this email reaches you in good health and spirits. This is Priscilla Garcia. I'm sure you remember me. I graduated with the 2012 class of OASIS with Frank Gil, Bobby Sosa, and a few other awesome students. I just wanted to reach out to you just to tell you that "I understand!" all that you did for us students in the OASIS program. You understood what it was like for us to struggle, all have different backgrounds, coming from different homes, having struggles at home that affected us in school and life. Some of us might have had short attentions spans even in high school. Some of us found it hard to sit a good while and try to do an assignment without dosing off. Some of us didn't have money for lunch. Some of us didn't have good days; some of us had great responsibilities regarding our families that made school work sadly our last priority. It felt like nobody knew what we were going through at home, until you came into our lives. Growing up sadly we all learn to judge people, the first day of school the students and I saw you and got kind of intimidated by you. We thought "They finally put us in a class with a man who looks like he's gonna be hard on us and might even yell at us about our school work." We very, very quickly noticed the pictures on the walls of you and all of your students smiling and in their graduation gowns with you right in the front with a bigger smile than any of the students. We saw that you had a fridge in your class, couches in the back of your class, and computers by the windows and most importantly you had a ton of positive reinforcement quotes around class.

We soon learned that the fridge was stocked with frozen burritos for students who didn't have lunch money, the couches in the back for students, mentors, and people visiting to have a nice seat to sit, a little sliding door behind the podium that had materials for the students whose families could not afford the folders, pencils, paper, and pens for their children. The computers by the windows were to help us learn how to type a resume for future jobs, teddy bears and stuffed animals that till this day I still have. And of course everybody's favorite, the cookies!! Thank you for all of those awesome and loving gestures because they made me who I am.

Can I tell you how you changed my life, Mr. LaVigne? They say that a parent's voice is what a child hears when they make choices on their own. Well, that wasn't the case for me. After graduation, I always heard your voice! "You reap what you sow." "You can do it if you set your mind to it."

Well, Mr. LaVigne, after graduation I was so happy to finally enroll into college and prove to everybody, especially my family, what I was capable of. I know I would not have graduated without you. Because it seemed like you were the only adult in my life that cared about my future. Mr. LaVigne, do you remember when I would be absent for days at a time? And a student told you that she saw me working at McDonalds? You thought that I was missing school to make money for my family? And it turned out to be my older sister working? The day I came back to school, you asked me if you could have a word with me outside. You then asked me if I'm missing school to go to work and I told you "No, Mr. LaVigne, that's my older sister." And we just both kind of giggled and said "Honest misunderstanding." Well, Mr. LaVigne, what I didn't tell you that day was that the girl working at McDonalds really was my

19-year-old sister, my sister who had a 2-and-a-half-year-old baby whose father was in jail. With my sister being a single mother and me being her only sibling, I wasn't missing school to go to work. I was missing school so she could go to work to provide for her son.

The days throughout my senior year that I was absent was because I was watching my nephew while my sister worked. I had been doing this for my sister since my nephew was 2 months old during my sophomore year. My mother was also working, doing her own things, unable to help with the baby. Nobody knew my secret. I kept it safe like it was against my religion to talk about it. Since my sophomore year, I missed so many days of school to help my sister raise her son. I was Mommy during the day when I should have been a student during the day. Nobody in my family really stopped to ask me about school or even when my graduation date was. The more I missed school to watch my nephew, the more I fell behind. By the time my senior year had come around, I was still in OASIS for my low GPA. So much has happened right after graduation.

After graduation, I took it upon myself to enroll myself into college. I was going to go to college with or without the help of my family. I would be the first in my family to go to college and fight for my education, reach for my goals, and achieve my dreams of being a successful young woman. A month after graduation, my mother told me, "If you can enroll yourself into college on your own and think you are an adult, then go into the world and see how it really is."

My mom kicked me out of the home I had grown up in. At only 17 years old I was kicked out of my house for enrolling myself into community college without my mother's approval. At the time, I had a boyfriend. I'm sure you remember me talking about him. His family was loving and kind enough to take me into their home and help me with school and transportation. They taught me how to drive, how to get to school, helped me get my license, and gave me the emotional support I needed to get into school and stay in school. When I enrolled myself into college, I specifically remembered the school asking me, "What would you like to major in?" And I thought to myself, "I want to change lives like Mr. LaVigne did. I want to make an impact." I asked to be placed in the teacher track and to major in child development because I thought to myself, "I will be these children's first teacher in their life. I can mold these children while they are young, and they will learn sooner." I took classes for 4 years full time 14 units a semester to get what I needed for my child development courses. Every class was one class closer to changing a life. While still living with my boyfriend, I kept my mind in the books and heart in the future. Four years ago, my boyfriend and I went our own ways on good terms. He left to the army and I stayed in school. I moved in with my dad whom I've never lived with my whole life, waking up early, going to school, and coming home late to do homework. I worked my mind, heart, and body till I had what I needed.

Next thing I knew, I had what I needed to be what I wanted and who I wanted. I was using the computer and resume skills that you taught me in your class on how to apply for a job as a preschool teacher. Before I knew it, it had all paid off. ALL OF IT! The days I spent in your class listening to your amazing stories about how you never let anything stop you! I always picture you mowing the lawn in a downpour of rain like that story you once told us. I never ever forgot it because that was me, but my version was me mowing down anything that was trying to stop me from being great, even in the storm and the rain. I learned to dance in it and keep my head held high because I was doing this for me and my future and nobody else.
Here I am 5 years later, a preschool teacher. Yes, a teacher! Because of YOU! I'm changing lives. I'm feeding kids who I know the families need help. I understand how your

students' problems didn't just stay in your class. They went home with you in your heart and mind; you felt for us and you did everything you could to help us. Even if some students didn't notice all you had given up to help us reach our goals. You kept us in your nest and you brought us food, comfort, positivity, life lessons, and the love that some of us did not get from our own homes and families. You truly just wanted the best for all of us. You always helped us emotionally even when you needed the emotional support yourself while your mother was sick. You are the most selfless human I have ever met till this day in my life, Mr. LaVigne. I'm so sorry that it took me so long to reach out to you. You probably would not believe me if I told you how often I think about the awesome way you have changed my life. When I look at my students and how small they are, I think about their future "Where will you be in 20 years?" "Who will you be in 20 years?" "What will you look like?" "Will I recognize you?"

I have so many families and parents who talk to me and cry to me about what their child and family is going through at home, and I finally understand how much it affects me. I drive home crying sometimes because I wish I could give these children the world. Some nights, I don't sleep because I wonder if my student Rossi's parents are fighting at home. I wonder if my student Natalia ate dinner. I wonder who's reading a book to Savannah. All of the little things matter to me, too.

I work with children and I make my class fun for them. I make school interesting. I make sure that all of my students know what love is. I make sure that my students get food. I also have a shelf in my class stocked with cookies for them. I learned so much from you, Mr. LaVigne. I'm here to tell you thank you so much for being who you are, because you are exactly who I needed in my life. I have no idea where I would be in this crazy world if it wasn't for you. I'm 22 years old working as a preschool teacher and living in my own little apartment just trying my best to change lives and be a light worker by sharing all the love in my heart and making this world a better place.

If I could say a few things to your new OASIS class, I would tell them that school should always come first! Learn to love yourself so much that you will make a better future for yourself. Listen to the stories Mr. LaVigne is sharing because all of the stories have hidden messages. Notice the genuine heart he has to offer. Learn to help others even if sometimes we can't help ourselves. Never give up, look at the big picture, and keep going forward. Also, pay attention to the sticks on top of the fridge that represent that working together makes people stronger. I can honestly say that all of those things I have learned from being in your class.

Thank you, Mr. LaVigne, for all that you have done for every single student who has been in your life. You truly are a blessing from God sent to help people in need. This world needs more people like you so please keep teaching students how to stay strong and to set goals and reach for the sky. I will be sending you photos of my students and class so that you can see the beautiful little faces of the lives that I am trying to touch. Please keep in contact, Mr. LaVigne, and thank you again for being my biggest fan and mentor. I needed somebody like you. Now I want to be the person that another child needs in their life. THANK YOU. THANK YOU. THANK YOU!!!

Your OASIS graduate of 2012,
Priscilla Garcia

Very few people get an opportunity to witness such extraordinary magnificence in their lives. Priscilla's beauty is adorned with unselfish devotion, courageous resilience, and genuine compassion. What a treasure she is! What a lucky person I am!

47

THEIR GIFT

*"Every man goes down to his death,
bearing in his hands only that
which he has given away."*

~ Persian Proverb

RYAN

I have a beautiful quilt on top of my bed. For the past twelve years, I have covered with it every night, and it has kept me warm and comforted, even during the summer. It is one of my most prized possessions. Tracy Fish, the mother of two former players of mine, made it for me years ago, and it is every bit as precious now as it was when she gave it to me.

Her younger son Ryan was a member of our football teams while I coached. He has Down syndrome, and playing football was an especially important thing in his life. We had to manage and closely monitor his involvement during practice and games, but he was a respected and loved member of our team. His physical and intellectual impairment prevented him from playing much in games, but we always put him in whenever we could.

Every year, we used to conclude spring football practice with an inter-squad game at our home stadium, Cal High. It was a big night because right after our Red & Gold Game, the annual Powder Puff Game (a game played by girl students and coached by our football payers) would take place. The stadium would always be packed. In that game every year, we let Ryan play a lot and actually carry the ball, scoring a touchdown. Ryan's touchdown run was always choreographed with all of our other players feigning missed tackles and falling backward as Ryan made his 70–80 yard gallop to the end zone. (We made sure that his touchdown run was a long one.) His mom videotaped it from the stands, and the entire crowd cheered loudly. The look on Ryan's face when he scored his touchdown each year was priceless and so was the total buy-in from all of our players! The look in his mother's eyes after the game was the greatest prize this coach has ever received. I was always so proud of our players and touched by these teammates who embraced Ryan and made him feel important and loved. They all congratulated Ryan after his touchdown, and those on defense told him how quick he was and how they "just couldn't get him." All those kids and everybody in the stands warmed my heart. Mrs. Fish was so happy and proud!

Ryan still attends all home varsity football games and stands in a section in the middle of the bleachers where he leads cheers and roots on our La Serna team.

The quilt given to Ken LaVigne by Tracy Fish,
the mother of two sons who played football for him at La Serna,
sits atop his bed and has been used every night for over twelve
years. It is one of his most-prized possessions.

AFTERWORD

"I've come to a frightening conclusion that
I am the decisive element in the classroom.
It's my personal approach that creates the climate.
It's my daily mood that makes the weather. As a
teacher, I possess a tremendous power to make a
child's life miserable or joyous. I can be a tool of torture
or an instrument of inspiration. I can humiliate or
heal. In all situations, it is my response that decides
whether a crisis will be escalated or de-escalated and
a child humanized or dehumanized."

~ Haim G. Ginott

Just as my grandmother did so many years ago, with this book, I have created *a quilt of words* intended for its beauty and comfort as much as it is for its utility. With stitches of profound experience, it was made to connect us all to something bigger than ourselves. Adversity and despair are common visitors to all people. These uninvited guests dig deeply into our hearts as we struggle to move forward to find meaning and happiness. Patches of cloth made from stories of hope and resilience adorn my quilt with the heroic magnificence of young lives that refused to surrender. Despite enduring frightening and seemingly impossible circumstances, these brave souls opened their hearts and minds to the possibility of a better life and the grueling path that would take them there. Their stories provide warmth and inspiration, illustrating what is possible when we all reach out to *coach the soul*.

ABOUT THE AUTHOR

KEN LAVIGNE

Ken LaVigne is a 2012 California State Teacher of the Year. In 2007, after almost thirty years as a successful high school football coach, Ken decided to retire from coaching and focus all of his attention on teaching. He was asked to develop a program to help his school's most at-risk students. He created a program called OASIS (Organized Academic Support In School) and recruited the finest students at La Serna High School to become academic mentors for their struggling classmates. Together, they created a program of support that is rooted in the application of core values that lead to success, not only in school, but in life. The results have been incredible with the great majority of these at-risk students graduating, continuing their education, and moving on to successful lives. Hundreds of teachers, counselors, and administrators have visited his classroom to witness, first hand, how this process works.

One of the greatest honors bestowed upon Ken LaVigne was having the COACH KEN LAVIGNE STRENGTH CENTER named after him with the words *COURAGE, CHARACTER* and *COMMITMENT* on the wall in big letters, exemplifying what he is really all about.

*Dash Verstegen, Ken LaVigne, and Andy George
at the dedication for La Serna's new weight training facility*

Ken and Gisele with sons Mark and Clint

Ken and Gisele have been married for 35 years. They are extremely proud of their sons, Mark and Clint. Gisele is a Senior Criminalist with the Los Angeles County Sheriff's Department, working in the Crime Lab. Mark and Clint are both UCLA graduates. Mark earned his Bachelor's Degree in Microbiology, Immunology, and Molecular Genetics from UCLA and a Master's Degree in Criminalistics from California State University, Los Angeles. He currently works for the Los Angeles County Sheriff's Department Crime Lab and teaches a class each fall in Forensic Science at California State University, Los Angeles. Clint earned his Bachelor's Degree in Communications from UCLA and is currently a Creative Executive in the entertainment industry.